Chronological and Background Charts of Church History

Chronological and Background Charts of Church History

ROBERT C. WALTON

with a foreword by Earle E. Cairns

ZondervanPublishingHouse

Grand Rapids, Michigan

A Division of HarperCollinsPublishers

CHRONOLOGICAL AND BACKGROUND CHARTS OF CHURCH HISTORY
Copyright © 1986 by The Zondervan Corporation,
Grand Rapids, Michigan.

Requests for information should be addressed to:
Zondervan Publishing House
Grand Rapids, Michigan 49530

Library of Congress Cataloging in Publication Data

Walton, Robert C. (Robert Charles)
    Chronological and background charts of church history.

    Bibliography: p.
    Includes index.
    1. Church history—Handbooks, manuals, etc. 2. Chronology,
Ecclesiastical—Handbooks, manuals.
BR146.W33 1985   270′.02′02   85-22559
ISBN 0-310-36281-4

Edited by Gerard Terpstra
Designed by Tom Hershberger

Printed in the United States of America

98 99 00 01 02 /CH/ 24 23 22 21 20 19 18 17

To D. Clair Davis,
who not only stimulated
my interest in church history
but also opened my eyes
to its practical applicability

Contents

THE MODERN EUROPEAN CHURCH (FROM 1648)

THE AMERICAN CHURCH (FROM 1607)

MISCELLANEOUS

Foreword

This is an era when people downgrade or ignore the value of both secular and sacred history. Cicero wisely said that those who know nothing of the past before their birth are doomed to be like children living in the present without the valuable wisdom of the past. Santayana believed that those who forget or ignore the past are doomed to repeat its least desirable features.

This should not be true of those who take advantage of the charts and diagrams presented in this book. Church history, because the church has existed for almost two thousand years and because it has a global scope, includes a mass of complex data. The author presents the significant facts of the past in useful charts and diagrams so that the student can see what facts are important and what their relationship is to the story of the church. The book will be a useful supplement to classroom text and lectures, supplying information on the who, what, when, where, and how of church history. It will also be useful to the general reader who desires a brief survey of the important data of church history.

EARLE E. CAIRNS
WHEATON, ILLINOIS

Preface

This collection of charts has a twofold purpose. The first purpose relates to the organization and accessibility of the factual information involved in the study of church history. As a church history teacher, I found that my greatest challenge lay in taking a vast amount of information and reducing it to some orderly form for the purpose of presenting it to my class. This book takes the process a step further, reducing what is often found in paragraph form to a series of charts. As such, I hope it will be helpful to student and teacher alike both as a way to gain rapid access to basic information without wading through many pages of text and as a way of providing orderly categories into which that information may be placed.

The second purpose relates to the interpretation and presentation of material. Many of these charts have developed out of my own teaching experience, and I trust they will be as useful to other teachers as they have been to me in presenting to students an interpretive overview of a particular trend or pattern or in providing a simple schema for grasping an especially knotty issue.

To the extent that the presentation of history is selective, it is also subjective. Nevertheless, I believe that my decisions concerning which people and facts to include and which to exclude have resulted in a collection of charts that will prove to be useful and enlightening to many people. I hope that this book may in some small measure stimulate not only understanding of, but also appreciation for, the study of church history, which is, after all, the chronicle of God's work in the world.

1. The Twelve Disciples After the Death of Jesus

NAME	BIBLICAL INFORMATION	TRADITIONAL INFORMATION
SIMON PETER	Preached sermon on Day of Pentecost. Healed lame man at gate of temple. Withstood persecution of Sanhedrin. Rebuked Ananias and Sapphira and Simon Magus. Raised Dorcas from the dead. Preached gospel to Cornelius. Miraculously delivered from prison. Rebuked by Paul at Antioch. Wrote two New Testament epistles.	Late traditions speak of visits to Britain and Gaul. Was crucified upside-down in Rome during Neronian persecution (A.D. 64–68).
ANDREW		Is supposed to have preached in Scythia, Asia Minor, and Greece. Was crucified at Patras in Achaia.
JAMES, SON OF ZEBEDEE	Was executed by Herod Agrippa I.	
JOHN	Participated in healing of lame man at temple. Followed up Philip's work in Samaria. Was exiled late in life on island of Patmos. Wrote Gospel, three epistles, and Apocalypse.	Ministered at Ephesus. Is said to have rebuked early Gnostic Cerinthus. Died a natural death in Ephesus c. A.D. 100.
PHILIP		Is said to have been crucified in Hierapolis in Asia Minor.
MATTHEW	Wrote Gospel that bears his name.	Conflicting traditions place him in Ethiopia, Parthia, Persia, and Macedonia.
THOMAS		Supposedly preached in Babylon. Strong early tradition tells of his founding churches and eventually being martyred in India.
BARTHOLOMEW		Is supposed to have accompanied Philip to Hierapolis. Was martyred after ministry in Armenia.
JAMES, SON OF ALPHAEUS		Has been persistently confused with James the brother of Jesus in early church tradition. Possibly ministered in Syria.
THADDAEUS		Has often been confused with Jude the brother of Jesus. Tradition associates his ministry with Edessa.
SIMON THE ZEALOT		Variously (and dubiously) associated with Persia, Egypt, Carthage, and Britain.
JUDAS ISCARIOT	Hanged himself after betraying Jesus.	

2. Early Symbols of Christianity

SYMBOL	SIGNIFICANCE
ALPHA–OMEGA	eternality of Christ
ANCHOR	faith
BREAD AND WINE	eucharist—death of Christ
CHI–RHO	first two letters of "Christ" in Greek
CROSS	death of Christ
DOVE	Holy Spirit at baptism of Christ
FIRE	Holy Spirit on Day of Pentecost
FISH	initial letters of "Jesus Christ, God's Son, Savior" in Greek, spelling ICHTHUS, the Greek word for "fish"; feeding of 5000; "fishers of men"
LAMB	Christ's self-sacrifice
SHEPHERD	Christ's care for His people
SHIP	Church (Noah's ark; cf. baptism)
VINE	Christ's union with His people; wine of eucharist

3. The Apostolic Fathers

NAME	DATES	PLACES OF MINISTRY	WRITINGS	NOTABLE FACTS
CLEMENT OF ROME	c.30–c.100	Rome	I Clement	Is considered by Roman Catholic church to have been 4th pope. Is perhaps mentioned in Phil. 4:3. Was martyred under Domitian. His letter stresses apostolic succession.
IGNATIUS	d. 117	Antioch in Syria	To the Ephesians To the Magnesians To the Trallians To the Romans To the Philadelphians To the Smyrnaeans To Polycarp	His letters were written en route to martyrdom in Rome—a fate he joyfully espoused. Was first to distinguish between bishops and elders. Opposed Gnostic heresies. Was martyred under Trajan.
HERMAS	late 1st to early 2nd century	Rome	The Shepherd	Was a contemporary of Clement. Wrote of visions and parables. Was perhaps a former slave. Was probably Jewish.
BARNABAS OF ALEXANDRIA	late 1st to early 2nd century	Alexandria	Epistle of Barnabas	Was probably an Alexandrian Jew. Was familiar with allegorical methods of Philo.
PAPIAS	c.60–c.130	Hierapolis	Exposition of the Oracles of Our Lord	Was an acquaintance of the apostle John. Held premillennial view of eschatology. Claimed Mark's Gospel was based on Peter's words. Said that Matthew's Gospel was originally written in Aramaic.
POLYCARP	c.69–160	Smyrna	Epistle to the Philippians	Was an acquaintance of the apostle John. Compiled and preserved epistles of Ignatius. Is said to have confronted Marcion as "the firstborn of Satan." Was martyred under Antoninus Pius.

4. The Second-Century Apologists

NAME	DATES	PLACES OF MINISTRY	REPRESENTATIVE WRITINGS (* = Lost)	NOTABLE FACTS
QUADRATUS	early 2nd century	Athens	Apology*	Was bishop of Athens. His *Apology* was addressed to Emperor Hadrian. Contrasts Christianity with Jewish and pagan worship.
ARISTIDES	early 2nd century	Athens	Apology*	His *Apology* was addressed to Emperor Hadrian. Shows strong Pauline influence.
JUSTIN MARTYR	c.100–165	Palestine Ephesus Rome	First Apology Second Apology Dialogue with Trypho the Jew Against Heresies* Against Marcion*	Was trained in philosophy. Was an itinerant lay teacher. Personally opposed Marcion. Developed concept of *logos spermaticos*. Argued for Christianity on basis of prophecy, miracles, and ethics. Was beheaded in Rome.
TATIAN	110–172	Assyria Syria Rome	Diatessaron To the Greeks	Was a pupil of Justin. Argued temporal priority of Christianity over other religions. Produced first harmony of Gospels. Later fell into Gnosticism. His followers were called Encratites.
ATHENAGORAS	2nd century	Athens	Apology On the Resurrection of the Dead	Was a Platonist. Wrote in classical style.
THEOPHILUS	d. 181	Antioch	To Autolycus	Was a severe polemicist against pagan philosophers. Was bishop of Antioch.
MELITO	d. 190	Sardis	about 20 works, all lost	Was bishop of Sardis. Supported Quartodecimans. Produced first Christian list of the books of the Old Testament.
HEGESIPPUS	2nd century	Syria Greece Rome	Memorials*	Was a converted Jew. Collected information on early history of church to prove its purity and apostolicity. Blamed all heresies on Judaism.

5. The Arguments of the Apologists

JEWISH ARGUMENTS VS. CHRISTIANITY	RESPONSES OF APOLOGISTS
Christianity is a deviant form of Judaism.	The Jewish law is by nature temporary and points to the new covenant.
The humble carpenter who died on a cross does not correspond to the Messiah prophesied in the Old Testament.	The Old Testament predicted both the sufferings and the glory of the Messiah.
The deity of Christ contradicts the unity of God.	The Old Testament indicates a plurality of persons within the unity of the Godhead.

APOLOGISTS' ARGUMENTS AGAINST JUDAISM

Old Testament prophecy is fulfilled in Christ.
Old Testament types point to Christ.
The destruction of Jerusalem showed God's condemnation of Judaism and vindication of Christianity.

PAGAN ARGUMENTS VS. CHRISTIANITY	RESPONSES OF APOLOGISTS
The doctrine of the Resurrection is absurd.	There were eyewitnesses in Gospels. The effect on disciples was profound. There is analogy in natural cycles (e.g., seasons).
There are contradictions in the Scriptures.	Harmonies like Tatian's *Diatessaron* answer contradictions.
Atheism is widely held.	Even Plato favored an unseen god.
Christianity is the worship of a criminal.	Jesus' trial violated law.
Christianity is a novelty.	Christianity had been in preparation for all eternity. Moses antedated pagan philosophers.
Christianity evidences a lack of patriotism.	Christians obey all laws that do not violate conscience.
Christians practice incest and cannibalism.	Observe the lifestyle of Christians, particularly examples of martyrs.
Christianity leads to the destruction of society.	Natural calamities are really the true God's judgment against false worship.

APOLOGISTS' ARGUMENTS AGAINST PAGANISM

Pagan philosophers plagiarized, stealing their best ideas from Moses and the prophets.
Polytheism is a philosophical absurdity and moral disaster.
Pagan philosophers contradict one another and even themselves.

APOLOGISTS' ARGUMENTS FOR CHRISTIANITY

All truth found in pagan philosophers anticipates Christianity and is brought together by it.
Miracles performed by Christ, the apostles, and other Christians prove its truth.
The spread of Christianity despite overwhelming obstacles shows it to be true.
Christianity alone is suited to meet the deepest needs of human beings.

6. The Third-Century Church Fathers

NAME	DATES	PLACES OF MINISTRY	REPRESENTATIVE WRITINGS (* = Lost)	NOTABLE FACTS
IRENAEUS	late 2nd century	Smyrna Gaul	Against Heresies On the Unity of God and the Origin of Evil	Studied under Polycarp. Was a missionary and apologist. Strong opponent of Gnosticism. Held premillennial views. Was bishop of Lyons. Was allegedly martyred in Lyons.
CLEMENT	c.150–c.215	Alexandria Antioch Jerusalem	Exhortation to the Greeks The Pedagogue Stromata	Was trained in philosophy. Was converted as an adult. Emphasized Logos. Approached Scripture allegorically. Wrote oldest extant Christian hymn, "Shepherd of Tender Youth."
TERTULLIAN	c.160–c.220	Carthage	Prescription of Heretics Against Marcion Against Praxeus	Was a son of Roman army officer. Was trained in law. Was converted in middle age. Joined Montanists c.200. Laid important groundwork for doctrine of Trinity.
HIPPOLYTUS	c.170–c.236	Rome	Philosophumena (Numerous lost commentaries)	Studied under Irenaeus. Opposed contemporary bishops of Rome. Used allegorical method of interpretation. Died in exile on Sardinia.

6. The Third-Century Church Fathers (continued)

NAME	DATES	PLACES OF MINISTRY	REPRESENTATIVE WRITINGS (* = Lost)	NOTABLE FACTS
JULIUS AFRICANUS	c.160–c.240	Palestine	Chronography	Studied under Origen. His historical research covered period from Creation to A.D. 221.
ORIGEN	c.185–c.254	Alexandria Caesarea	Hexapla Against Celsus De Principiis	His father Leonidas was martyred in 202. Studied under Clement. Succeeded Clement as catechist in 203. Was a notable advocate of allegorical interpretation of Scripture. Was extremely ascetic. Was exiled by his enemies in the church. Died after torture at hands of Romans.
CYPRIAN	c.200–258	Carthage	Unity of the Church De Lapsis	Was trained in rhetoric. Was converted in 245. Was bishop of Carthage from 247. Was influenced by Tertullian. Emphasized authority of episcopate. Took strict stand against those who faltered under persecution. Was martyred under Valerian.
GREGORY THAUMATURGOS	c.213–270	Palestine Asia Minor	Declaration of Faith Eulogy on Origen	Was converted by and studied under Origen. Was known as the Wonder-Worker. Was bishop of Neo-Caesarea.

7. The Development of the New Testament Canon

PERIOD	CHARACTER-ISTICS	APPROXIMATE DATES	SIGNIFICANT SOURCES	BOOKS RECEIVED	BOOKS QUESTIONED
APOSTOLIC FATHERS	No serious debate, no official pro-nouncements	100–140	quotations in Apostolic Fathers	Four Gospels Pauline Epistles (unspecified corpus)	None
GNOSTIC OPPOSITION	reaction against Gnos-tic truncation of canon (esp. writings of Marcion)	140–220	quotations in Church Fathers Muratorian Canon (c.180) Gospel of Truth (Gnostic)	Four Gospels Acts 13 Pauline Epistles 1 Peter 1 John Jude Revelation	Hebrews James 2 Peter 2–3 John Shepherd of Hermas Didache Revelation of Peter
FINAL SOLIDIFI-CATION	general agree-ment by end of fourth century	220–400	Origen	Four Gospels Acts 13 Pauline Epistles 1 Peter 1 John Revelation	Hebrews James 2 Peter 2–3 John Jude Shepherd of Hermas Didache
			Eusebius	Four Gospels Acts 14 Pauline Epistles 1 Peter 1 John	James 2 Peter 2–3 John Jude Revelation Shepherd of Hermas Didache
			Athanasius (Paschal letter of 367—final accept-ance in East)	Present Canon	
			Synod of Rome (382—final acceptance in West)	Present Canon	
			Synod of Carthage (397—acceptance by entire church)	Present Canon	

8. Books Debated for Inclusion in the New Testament Canon

QUESTIONED BOOK	REASONS GIVEN FOR ACCEPTANCE	REASONS GIVEN FOR EXCLUSION	RESULT
HEBREWS	Thought Pauline in East	Thought non-Pauline forgery in West	Accepted
JAMES	Thought genuine in East	Authorship questioned in West	Accepted
2 PETER	Petrine authorship	Authorship questioned Similarity of chapter 2 to Jude	Accepted
2–3 JOHN	Johannine authorship	Lack of citations in early writings	Accepted
JUDE	Early citations Apostolic authorship	Authorship questioned	Accepted
REVELATION	Widely recognized as Johannine	Questioned by Eusebius largely because of his opposition to chiliasm	Accepted
THE SHEPHERD OF HERMAS	Edifying contents Visions from God	Nonapostolic origin Late date	Excluded
DIDACHE	Record of genuine apostolic traditions	Uncertain origin Late date	Excluded
REVELATION OF PETER	Suspected Petrine authorship Similarity to Johannine Apocalypse	Authenticity doubted	Excluded

9. Ante-Nicene Heresies

HERESY	LEADING TEACHERS	HISTORICAL INFORMATION	CHARACTERISTIC TEACHINGS
EBIONISM (Elkesaites, Mandaeans)		Originated in Palestine in the late 1st century, later spread to Asia Minor. Was made up mostly of Jewish Christians. Used Gospel of Matthew in Hebrew.	Taught universality of Mosaic law (needed for salvation). Advocated antipathy to Paul. Jesus acknowledged as the Messiah, but only as a man on whom the Spirit came at His baptism. Looked for imminent Millennium.
GNOSTICISM	Simon Magus (1st century) Cerinthus (late 1st century) Basilides (early 2nd century) Saturninus (early 2nd century) Marcion (d. c.160) Valentinus (d. c.160) Tatian (110–172)	Had roots in pagan philosophy, especially Platonism. Was influenced by Oriental mysticism. Had little appeal to masses; most influential among church leaders. Appeared throughout Empire. Worship ranged from very simple to very elaborate. Forced church to formulate rules of faith and New Testament canon. Caused church to emphasize apostolic succession as repository of truth.	Thought themselves possessors of unique higher insight ("gnosis"). Thought themselves of spirit, other people of soul or body. Taught matter is evil. Held to hierarchy of aeons (pleroma). Produced either sensuality or asceticism. Was dualistic. Generally rejected Old Testament and Judaism. Used allegorical interpretation. Said world was created by Demiurge (= Jehovah). Believed Christ's body was an illusion.
MONTANISM	Montanus (2nd century) Priscilla (2nd century) Maximilla (2nd century) Tertullian (c.160–c.220)	Originated in Phrygia. Later spread to Rome and North Africa.	Were ascetic. Were chiliastic. Expected imminent start of Millennium. Practiced glossolalia. Were generally orthodox in doctrine. Thought themselves spiritual, others carnal. Continued prophetic revelation. Held to universal priesthood of believers. Opposed art of any kind. Sought martyrdom.
MANICHAEISM	Mani (215–277)	Originated in Persia. Contains many elements of Zoroastrianism. Mani was flayed alive, his skin stuffed and hung over city gate in Persia. Augustine was a follower early in life. Is similar to later Paulicians, Bogomils, Cathari, Albigensians. Was characterized by strict hierarchical organization.	Held dualistic view of creation (light vs. darkness). Believed Christ was representative of light, Satan of darkness. Said apostles corrupted Christ's teaching, Mani revealed it in pure form. Taught that Christ's body was illusory. Followers were severely ascetic.

10. Roman Persecutions of Christians

DATES	EMPEROR	NATURE AND EXTENT OF PERSECUTION	NOTABLE MARTYRS
64	Nero	Took place in Rome and vicinity only. Christians were made scapegoats for burning Rome. Sadistic measures included burning Christians alive to illuminate Nero's gardens.	Paul Peter
c.90–96	Domitian	Was capricious, sporadic, centered in Rome and Asia Minor. Christians were persecuted for refusal to offer incense to the genius of the emperor.	Clement of Rome John (exiled to Patmos)
98–117	Trajan	Was sporadically enforced. Christians were lumped with other groups whose patriotism was considered suspect. Christians were to be executed when found, but not sought out.	Ignatius Symeon Zozimus Rufus
117–138	Hadrian	Was sporadically enforced. Policies of Trajan were continued. Any who brought false witness against Christians were to be punished.	Telesphorus
161–180	Marcus Aurelius	Emperor was a Stoic who opposed Christianity on philosophical grounds. Christians were blamed for natural disasters.	Justin Martyr Pothinus Blandina
202–211	Septimus Severus	Conversion to Christianity was forbidden.	Leonidas Irenaeus Perpetua
235–236	Maximinus the Thracian	Christian clergy were ordered executed. Christians were opposed because they had supported emperor's predecessor, whom he had assassinated.	Ursula Hippolytus
249–251	Decius	Was first empire-wide persecution. Offering of incense to genius of emperor was demanded. Enthusiastic return to paganism required utter extermination of Christianity.	Fabianus Alexander of Jerusalem
257–260	Valerian	Christians' property was confiscated Christians were prohibited right of assembly	Origen Cyprian Sixtus II
303–311	Diocletian Galerius	This was worst persecution of all. Churches were destroyed, Bibles burned. All civil rights of Christians were suspended. Sacrifice to gods was required.	Mauritius Alban

11. Nicene and Post-Nicene Fathers

NAME	DATES	PLACES OF MINISTRY	REPRESENTATIVE WRITINGS	NOTABLE FACTS
LACTANTIUS	c.240–320	Italy Gaul	Divine Institutes	Was born of pagan parents. Was converted as an adult. Served as tutor to Constantine's son.
EUSEBIUS	c.263– c.339	Caesarea	Ecclesiastical History Chronicle Life of Constantine	Known as father of church history. Taught at theological school in Caesarea. Became bishop of Caesarea, refused Antioch patriarchate. Sought compromise in Arian controversy, opposing both Arius and Athanasius. Was friend and advisor of Constantine. Held antichiliastic views.
HILARY	c.291–371	Poitiers	On the Trinity	Was converted late in life. Was greatest Western opponent of Arianism. Was named bishop of Poitiers in 350.
ATHANASIUS	c.296–373	Alexandria	On the Incarnation of the Divine Word Orations against the Arians Against Apollinarius	Was most noted defender of Trinitarian orthodoxy. Became secretary to bishop Alexander of Alexandria. Was vocal participant in Council of Nicea. Was named patriarch of Alexandria in 328. Was exiled five times. Lived ascetic life.
BASIL	c.329–379	Cappadocia	Five books against Eunomius	Was raised in Christian home. Studied philosophy in Athens. Lived ascetic life. Became bishop of Caesarea in Cappadocia. Opposed Arianism. Founded hospital for lepers.

11. Nicene and Post-Nicene Fathers (continued)

NAME	DATES	PLACES OF MINISTRY	REPRESENTATIVE WRITINGS	NOTABLE FACTS
GREGORY OF NYSSA	c.330–c.394	Cappadocia	Against Eunomius Against Apollinarius On the Deity of the Son and the Holy Ghost	Was brother of Basil. Was influenced by Origen. Was an allegorist. Lived ascetic life, though he did marry. Reluctantly became bishop of Nyssa in 372. Opposed Arianism. Was first to stress distinction between substance and persons in Trinity. Participated in Council of Constantinople.
GREGORY OF NAZIANZUS	c.330–c.390	Cappadocia Constantinople	Theological Orations	Was son of bishop of Nazianzus. Studied with Basil in Athens. Lived ascetic life. Became bishop of Nazianzus (374), then patriarch of Constantinople (381), but quickly resigned. Opposed Arianism. Was notable orator and poet.
AMBROSE	c.340–397	Milan	On Faith On the Holy Ghost On the Sacraments	Was son of governor of Gaul. Prepared for civil service. Became praetor of North Italy. Was acclaimed bishop of Milan in 374 before baptism. Lived ascetic life. Opposed Arianism. Withstood Emperor Theodosius over massacre of Thessalonians. Influenced Augustine through sermons.
JOHN CHRYSOSTOM	c.374–407	Antioch Constantinople	On the Priesthood Homilies	Chrysostom, his nickname, means "Golden Mouth." Was greatest preacher of ancient church. Stressed ethical application in sermons. Was son of Roman officer. Studied rhetoric. Preferred monastic life. Became patriarch of Constantinople in 397. Was banished by Empress Eudoxia. Died in exile.

11. Nicene and Post-Nicene Fathers (continued)

NAME	DATES	PLACES OF MINISTRY	REPRESENTATIVE WRITINGS	NOTABLE FACTS
JEROME	c.345–420	Rome Antioch Bethlehem	Vulgate Catalogue of Illustrious Authors (Numerous commentaries)	Was born into Christian family. Was educated in rhetoric. Was tireless advocate of monasticism. Spent years in desert seclusion. Was one of few Christians in his age who knew Hebrew. Became secretary to Damasus, bishop of Rome. Encouraged many Roman women toward asceticism. Lived his last 35 years in Bethlehem. His Latin Vulgate later became the official Bible of the Roman Catholic Church.
THEODORE OF MOPSUESTIA	c.350–428	Antioch Mopsuestia	Commentary on the Minor Prophets Against the Allegorists Against Defenders of Original Sin	Was father of Antiochan theology. Was a friend of Chrysostom. Abandoned monastic life to marry. Was named bishop of Mopsuestia in 392. Stressed grammatical-historical context for interpretation of Scripture. Opposed allegorical interpretation of Scripture. Was teacher of Nestorius. Was condemned by Second Council of Constantinople.
AUGUSTINE	354–430	North Africa	Confessions Meditations The City of God Enchiridion Retractationes	Was born to pagan father and Christian mother. Studied philosophy at Carthage. Espoused Manichaean heresy early in life. Was converted in Milan in 386. Was influenced by Ambrose. Was named bishop of Hippo in 395. Espoused mild form of asceticism. Opposed Manichaeans, Donatists, Pelagians. Wrote first Christian philosophy of history. His work was used to support both sides of almost every medieval theological debate.
CYRIL	376–444	Alexandria	Against Nestorius Against Julian the Apostate	Was champion of Alexandrian theology. Became patriarch of Alexandria c.412. Used force and duplicity against his opponents, both Christians and others. Opposed Chrysostom, Theodore, Nestorius. Advocated veneration of Mary.

12. Development of Episcopacy in the First Five Centuries

PERIOD	SOURCES	DESCRIPTION
1st century	New Testament	Elder-bishops and deacons in each church were under the supervision of the apostles.
Early 2nd century	Ignatius	Elders and bishops were differentiated. Each congregation was governed by bishop, elders, and deacons.
Late 2nd century	Irenaeus Tertullian	Diocesan bishops—a bishop now oversaw a group of congregations in a geographical area; they were thought to be successors of the apostles.
Mid-3rd century	Cyprian	Priesthood and sacrifice. Elders (presbyteros) come to be seen as sacrificing priests. Primacy of bishop of Rome was asserted.
Early 4th century	Council of Nicea	Metropolitan bishops (archbishops) by virtue of their location in population centers gained ascendancy over *chorepiscopi* (country bishops).
Late 4th century	Council of Constantinople	Patriarchs. Special honor was given to the bishops of Rome, Alexandria, Antioch, Constantinople, and Jerusalem. Patriarch of Constantinople was given primacy next to the bishop of Rome.
Mid-5th century	Leo I Council of Chalcedon	The supremacy of Rome—Leo I claimed authority over the whole church on the basis of succession from Peter.

13. Factors Contributing to the Supremacy of the Bishop of Rome

FACTOR	RESULT
MATTHEW 16:17–19	Papal claims rest on the assertion that Peter was given authority by Jesus over the entire church. This claim was first made by Leo I.
APOSTOLIC SUCCESSION	The teaching that the apostles passed on their authority to their successors led to the conclusion that Peter's supreme authority had been perpetuated in the bishops of Rome.
MARTYRDOM OF PETER AND OF PAUL	With the rise of the veneration of martyred saints, Rome gained prestige as the site of the deaths of the two principal apostles. The persecution under Nero also gave to the Roman church a special prominence by virtue of its suffering.
POPULATION OF ROME	Both the size of the city and the size of the church contributed to the authority of the bishop.
IMPERIAL CAPITAL	After the Edict of Milan, the emperors often sought advice on religious matters from the bishops of Rome.
LANGUAGE	The Latin-speaking West, led by the bishop of Rome, was often able to cut through the knotty theological dilemmas that incapacitated the Greek-speaking East, because of the lesser ability of the Latin language to express subtle shades of meaning.
LOCATION	Of the five patriarchal cities, only Rome was in the West; thus the bishop of Rome exercised authority over much more territory than the other patriarchs did.
MISSIONARY OUTREACH	The bishops of Rome, such as Gregory I, encouraged successful missionary work among the barbarian tribes, who then looked to Rome with great respect. The Eastern patriarchs were much less successful in evangelizing the Persians and later the Muslims.
BARBARIAN INVASIONS	The collapse of the Western Empire under the barbarian invasions left the church as the major integrating force in society—in the empire as well as among the "Christian" barbarians.
MUSLIM CONQUEST	The loss of the territories of the patriarchs of Antioch, Alexandria, and Jerusalem to Islam and the continual pressure exerted against Constantinople also increased the authority of the Roman bishop.

14. Major Ancient Church Doctrinal Controversies

CONTROVERSY	MAJOR HERETICAL LEADERS	MAJOR ORTHODOX LEADERS	RELEVANT COUNCILS	ACCEPTED CONCLUSIONS
TRINITARIAN CONTROVERSY	Arius Eusebius of Nicomedia	Athanasius Hosius Basil the Great Gregory of Nyssa Gregory of Nazianzus Augustine of Hippo	Nicea (325) Constantinople (381)	Christ is "of same substance with the Father." Father, Son, and Spirit are "coeternal, consubstantial, and coequal."
CHRISTOLOGICAL CONTROVERSY	Apollinarius Nestorius Eutyches	Cyril of Alexandria Theodoret Leo I	Constantinople (381) Ephesus (431) Ephesus ("Robber Synod") (449) Chalcedon (451)	Christ is "one person in two natures, unmixed, unchanged, undivided, inseparable." Mary is "the Mother of God."
DONATIST CONTROVERSY	Donatus	Caecilian Augustine of Hippo	Arles (314)	"Outside the church there is no salvation."
PELAGIAN CONTROVERSY	Pelagius Coelestius John Cassian Caesarius of Arles	Augustine of Hippo Jerome	Ephesus (431) Orange (529)	Semi-Augustinianism; sacramental grace enables people to overcome their innate sinfulness.

15. Ancient Church Trinitarian Heresies

HERESY	MAJOR PROPONENTS	SUMMARY
MONARCHIANISM (Adoptionism)	Theodotus of Byzantium Paul of Samosata	Jesus became Christ at His baptism, was adopted by the Father after His death.
SABELLIANISM (Modalism, Patripassionism)	Sabellius Praxeus	One God reveals Himself in three ways.
ARIANISM	Arius Eusebius of Nicomedia Eudoxius Eunomius	Christ is the first created being.
SEMI-ARIANISM (Eusebianism)	Basil of Ancyra Gregory of Laodicea	Christ is of similar essence with the Father but is subordinate to Him.
MACEDONIANISM (Pneumatomachism)	Macedonius	The Holy Spirit is a created being.

16. Ancient Church Christological Heresies

HERESY	MAJOR PROPONENTS	SUMMARY
APOLLINARIANISM	Apollinarius	Christ had no human spirit. The Logos replaced it.
NESTORIANISM	Nestorius	The Logos indwelt the person of Jesus, making Christ a God-bearing man rather than the God-Man. Affirmed merely mechanical rather than organic union of the person of Christ.
EUTYCHIANISM	Eutyches	The human nature of Christ was absorbed by the Logos.
MONOPHYSITISM	Severus Julian of Halicarnassus Stephanus Niobes	Christ had one nature (unwilling to accept impersonal human nature of Christ)
MONOTHELITISM	Theodore of Arabia Sergius Cyrus of Alexandria	Christ had no human will, just the one divine will.

17. The Pelagian Controversy

POSITION	MAJOR PROPONENTS	SUMMARY
PELAGIANISM	Pelagius Julian of Eclanum Coelestius	Man is born essentially good and capable of doing what is necessary for salvation.
AUGUSTINIANISM	Augustine of Hippo	Man is dead in sin; salvation is totally by the grace of God, which is given only to the elect.
SEMI-PELAGIANISM	John Cassian	The grace of God and the will of man work together in salvation, in which man must take the initiative.
SEMI-AUGUSTINIANISM	Caesarius of Arles	The grace of God comes to all, enabling a person to choose and perform what is necessary for salvation.

18. The Ecumenical Councils of the Early Church

LOCATION	DATE	EMPEROR	KEY PARTICIPANTS	MAJOR OUTCOMES
NICEA	325	Constantine	Arius Alexander Eusebius of Nicomedia Eusebius of Caesarea Hosius Athanasius	Declared Son *homoousios* (coequal, consubstantial, and coeternal) with Father. Condemned Arius. Drafted original form of Nicene Creed.
CONSTANTINOPLE	381	Theodosius	Meletius Gregory of Nazianzus Gregory of Nyssa	Confirmed results of Council of Nicea. Produced revised Nicene Creed. Ended Trinitarian Controversy. Affirmed deity of the Holy Spirit. Condemned Apollinarianism.
EPHESUS	431	Theodosius II	Cyril Nestorius	Declared Nestorianism heretical. Accepted by implication Alexandrian Christology. Condemned Pelagius.
CHALCEDON	451	Marcian	Leo I Dioscurus Eutyches	Declared Christ's two natures unmixed, unchanged, undivided, inseparable. Condemned Eutychianism.
CONSTANTINOPLE	553	Justinian	Eutychius	Condemned "Three Chapters" to gain support of Monophysites. Affirmed Cyrillian interpretation of Chalcedon.
CONSTANTINOPLE	680–681	Constantine IV		Rejected Monothelitism. Condemned Pope Honorius (d. 638) as heretical.
NICEA	787	Constantine VI		Declared veneration of icons and statues legitimate.

19. The Conversion of the Barbarian Tribes

TRIBE	DATE OF CONVERSION	KEY MISSIONARIES AND RULERS
GOTHS	c.340	Ulfilas (Arian)
	c.720	Boniface (Wynfrith) (Catholic)
PICTS	c.400	Ninian
IRISH	c.435	Patrick
FRANKS	c.496	Clovis
SCOTS	c.563	Columba
ANGLES AND SAXONS	c.600	Augustine of Canterbury Ethelbert
FRISIANS	c.690	Willibrord

20. Church and State, 754–1309

PERIOD	DATES	KEY EVENTS	LEADING FIGURES	CHARACTERISTICS
Holy Roman Empire of Charlemagne	754–962	754—Donation of Pepin mid-8th century—Donation of Constantine (forged) 800—crowning of Charlemagne mid-9th century—Pseudo-Isidorean Decretals (forged) 840—division of Empire among Charlemagne's grandsons	Pepin the Short (c.714–768) Charlemagne (742–814) Nicholas I (c.800–868)	Creation of Papal States made pope a temporal ruler. Crowning of Charlemagne set stage for power struggle between church and state. Feudal fragmentation of society occurred. In latter part of period, papacy was held by unworthy men under domination of Roman barons.
Holy Roman Empire of Otto I	962–1059	962—Otto I crowned Holy Roman Emperor by pope 1044–1046—papal schism 1054—schism of Eastern and Western churches	Otto I (912–973) Leo IX (1002–1054)	Period was characterized by constant German interference in Italian and papal affairs. Popes were generally weak, puppets of Italian or German overlords. Growth of Cluny reform developed strong leadership for church.
Increase of Papal Domination	1059–1216	1059—papal elections entrusted to College of Cardinals 1077—Henry IV humbled at Canossa 1095—Crusades begin 1122—Concordat of Worms 1215—Fourth Lateran Council	Hildebrand (Gregory VII) (c.1021–1085) Urban II (1042–1099) Henry IV (1050–1106) Innocent III (1161–1216)	Hildebrandine reform greatly enhanced power of papacy. Lay investiture controversy reached its peak. Excommunication and interdict became potent weapons in papal arsenal. Papal power reached its zenith as Innocent III claims absolute spiritual and temporal authority.
Decline of Papal Domination	1216–1309	1291—Fall of Acre, end of Crusades 1302—papal bull *Unam Sanctum* 1309—beginning of Babylonian Captivity; papacy moved to Avignon, France	Boniface VIII (c.1234–1303) Philip IV (the Fair) (1268–1314)	Popes continued to make grandiose claims of temporal power but were less and less able to back them up. By the end of the period, the papacy fell completely under French domination.

21. Early Medieval Church Leaders

NAME	DATES	PLACES OF MINISTRY	REPRESENTATIVE WRITINGS	NOTABLE FACTS
BOETHIUS	c.480–524	Athens Italy	Consolation of Philosophy Opuscula Sacra	Served in court of Arian Ostrogoth king Theodoric. Saw philosophy as able to lead man to God. Was executed when accused of treason.
GREGORY THE GREAT	540–604	Rome	Magna Moralia Dialogues	Was born into aristocratic family. Entered Benedictine monastery. Was first monk to become bishop of Rome. Asserted authority of bishop of Rome over entire Western church. Constructed popular theology that influenced medieval church. Stimulated missionary effort in England. Protected Rome against Lombards.
ISIDORE	c.560–636	Seville	Scripture Allegories The Catholic Faith Defended Against the Jews Etymologies Three Books of Sentences	Was named Archbishop of Seville (600). Headed Council of Toledo (633). Was alleged in Middle Ages to be compiler of Pseudo-Isidorean Decretals.
BEDE	c.673–735	Northumbria	Ecclesiastical History of England Life of St. Guthbert of Lindisfarne	Lived in monasteries from age 7. Never traveled more than a few miles from his birthplace. Gained most knowledge solely from monastery library.

21. Early Medieval Church Leaders (continued)

NAME	DATES	PLACES OF MINISTRY	REPRESENTATIVE WRITINGS	NOTABLE FACTS
JOHN OF DAMASCUS	c.675–749	Damascus Palestine	Orations Fount of Knowledge	Was born to Christian parents. Served in court of Islamic caliph. Supported icon worship. Later left caliph's service to enter monastery. Produced a theology normative for Eastern church.
ALCUIN	735–804	York Aachen Tours	The Trinity Life of St. Willibrord	Was born into aristocratic family. Was educated at Cathedral School of York. Later became master of Cathedral School. Summoned as tutor to Charlemagne's court. Opposed adoptionists. Revised Jerome's Vulgate.
PASCHASIUS RADBERTUS	c.785–865	Soissons Saxony	The Body and Blood of the Lord The Birth by the Virgin	Was orphaned as young child. Entered Benedictine monastery. Was a proponent of doctrine of transubstantiation. Was a friend of Louis the Pious. Opposed Gottschalk.
GOTTSCHALK	805–868	Rheims	The Eclogue of Theodolus	Was sent to monastery by parents as a child. As an adult, tried to leave monastery but was not permitted to do so. Defended Augustinian doctrine of predestination, for which he was condemned and imprisoned. Was treated brutally, died after 20 years in prison, was denied Christian burial.
JOHN SCOTUS ERIGENA	c.810–c.877	Ireland France	On Predestination On the Division of Nature	Was born in Ireland. Served in court of Charles the Bald in France. Was a Neoplatonist with pantheistic tendencies. Participated in predestinarian and Eucharistic controversies.

22. The Primary Causes of the East-West Schism of 1054

CAUSE	EASTERN CHURCH	WESTERN CHURCH
POLITICAL RIVALRY	Byzantine Empire	Holy Roman Empire
CLAIMS OF PAPACY	Patriarch of Constantinople was considered second in primacy to bishop of Rome.	Bishop of Rome claimed supremacy over entire church.
THEOLOGICAL DEVELOPMENT	Stagnated after Council of Chalcedon.	Continued to change and grow through controversies and expansion.
FILIOQUE CONTROVERSY	Declared that the Holy Spirit proceeds from the Father.	Declared that the Holy Spirit proceeds from the Father and the Son.
ICONOCLASTIC CONTROVERSY	Engaged in 120-year dispute over the use of icons in worship; finally concluded they could be used (statues prohibited).	Made constant attempts to interfere in what was purely an Eastern dispute (statues permitted).
DIFFERENCES IN LANGUAGE AND CULTURE	Greek/Oriental	Latin/Occidental
CLERICAL CELIBACY	Lower clergy were permitted to marry.	All clergy were required to be celibate.
OUTSIDE PRESSURES	Muslims constricted and put continual pressure on Eastern church.	Western Barbarians were Christianized and assimilated by Western church.
MUTUAL EXCOMMU-NICATION OF 1054	Michael Cerularius anathematized Pope Leo IX after having been excommunicated by him.	Leo IX excommunicated Patriarch Michael Cerularius of Constantinople.

23. The Crusades

CRUSADE	DATES	CHIEF MOTIVATORS	NOTABLE PARTICIPANTS	GOAL	RESULTS
FIRST CRUSADE	1096–1099	Urban II Peter the Hermit	Walter Sansavoir Peter the Hermit Gottschalk Raymund of Toulouse Godfrey Tancred Robert of Normandy	Liberation of Jerusalem from Turks	Crusaders captured Nicea, Antioch, Edessa, Jerusalem; established feudal Crusader kingdoms.
SECOND CRUSADE	1147–1148	Bernard of Clairvaux Eugene III	Konrad III Louis VII	Retake Edessa from Turks	Mistrust between Western Crusaders and Eastern guides led to decimation of Crusader army; attempt to take Damascus failed.
THIRD CRUSADE	1189–1192	Alexander III	Frederick Barbarossa Philip Augustus Richard I	Retake Jerusalem from Saladin and the Saracens	Frederick drowned; Philip returned home; Richard captured Acre and Joppa, made treaty with Saladin, and was captured and imprisoned in Austria on the way home.
FOURTH CRUSADE	1200–1204	Innocent II	Thibaut of Champagne Louis of Blois Baldwin of Flanders Simon De Montfort Henry Dandolo	Undermine Saracen power by invading Egypt	Christian city of Zara was sacked to repay Venice for transportation; for this the Crusaders were excommunicated; they then sacked Constantinople.
CHILDREN'S CRUSADE	1212	Nicholas Stephen		Supernatural conquest of Holy Land by "the pure in heart."	Most of the children were drowned at sea, sold into slavery, or slaughtered.
FIFTH CRUSADE	1219–1221	Honorius III	William of Holland John of Brienne	Undermine Saracen power by invading Egypt	Crusaders succeeded in taking Damietta in Egypt but soon lost it again.
SIXTH CRUSADE	1229		Frederick II	Regain Jerusalem	Crusaders made treaty with sultan, giving Frederick control of Jerusalem. Frederick was excommunicated for this.
SEVENTH CRUSADE	1248		Louis IX	Relief of Holy Land through invasion of Egypt	Crusaders were defeated in Egypt.

24. The Muslim Conquest and the Crusades—A Comparison

AREA OF COMPARISON	MUSLIM CONQUEST	CRUSADES
DATES	633–732	1095–1291
INITIATION	Death of Muhammad	Council of Clermont
TERMINATION	Battle of Tours	Fall of Acre
MOTIVATION	They desired to spread the true faith among the infidels by means of Jihad, or Holy War.	They sought to protect pilgrims and the glory of God and to recapture the holy places of Christendom from the infidel Turks.
INDUCEMENTS OFFERED	Immediate entrance to Paradise promised to those who die.	Plenary indulgence was offered—forgiveness of sins past, present, and future; for those who died, immediate entrance into heaven; for all others, forgiveness of debts and freedom from taxation.
TREATMENT OF ENEMIES	Pagans were required to convert or die; Jews and Christians were allowed to keep their religion but were required to pay tribute and refrain from proselytizing.	Conquered Muslims were indiscriminately put to the sword; inhabitants of Jewish ghettoes were slaughtered.
RESULTS	Palestine, Syria, Asia Minor, Egypt, North Africa, Spain were subjugated; Greek learning was preserved through "Dark Ages."	No permanent territorial gains were made; classical Greek and Roman culture was rediscovered; there was increased enmity between Eastern and Western churches and among Christians, Jews, and Muslims.

25. Arguments for the Existence of God—the Five Ways of Thomas Aquinas

ARGUMENT	OBSERVATIONS	IMPLICATIONS	CONCLUSION
FROM MOTION	Motion cannot initiate itself but must be motivated by something already in motion.	An infinite chain of movers is impossible, for then there would be no first mover and therefore no motion at all. The chain must have a beginning.	The unmoved Prime Mover is what we call God.
FROM CAUSALITY	Certain events are caused by prior events, which are themselves caused, etc.	As above, the causal chain cannot be infinite.	The uncaused First Cause is what we call God.
FROM POSSIBILITY	Certain things are transitory, their existence derivative. Their existence is possible rather than necessary.	The chain of derivative existence cannot be infinite but must find its source in a self-existent necessary Being.	This self-existent necessary Being is what we call God.
FROM IMPERFECTION	We judge certain things to have a lesser degree of perfection than others.	Relative assessments require an absolute standard of perfection. According to Aristotle, that which is greatest in truth is greatest in Being.	This absolute standard, God, must exist.
FROM DESIGN	Inanimate things function together to accomplish an ordered purpose.	This cannot occur by chance but requires an intelligent Designer.	This Designer is what we call God.

26. The Theology of Scholasticism

NAME	DATES	PLACES OF MINISTRY	REPRESENTATIVE WORKS	VIEW OF RELATIONSHIP OF FAITH AND REASON	VIEW OF NATURE OF UNIVERSALS	NOTABLE FACTS
ANSELM	1033–1109	Italy France Canterbury	Monologium Proslogium Cur Deus Homo	"Faith precedes knowledge."	Realist—*universalia ante rem*	Was born in Italy. Entered monastery in France. Became Archbishop of Canterbury (1093). Opposed lay investiture. Devised ontological argument for the existence of God. Promulgated substitutionary view of Atonement.
PETER ABELARD	1079–1142	France	Sic Et Non Christian Theology Story of Misfortunes	"Nothing is to be believed until it is understood."	Moderate Realist—*universalia in re*	In early years had disputes with most of his teachers. Became head of cathedral school in Paris. Fathered child out of wedlock with Heloise. Was castrated by order of her uncle. Retired to monastery. Was condemned as heretic by instigation of Bernard of Clairvaux.
BERNARD OF CLAIRVAUX	c.1090–1153	France	Degrees of Humility and Pride Loving God	"God is known so far as He is loved."	Mystic—this not an issue	Was born of noble parents. Entered Cistercian monastery (1113). Founded monastery in Clairvaux. In preaching encouraged Second Crusade. Was vehement opponent of Abelard. Was a noted hymn-writer.
PETER LOMBARD	1095–c.1159	Italy Paris	Four Books of Sentences	Dilemmas of faith to be resolved by reason.	Moderate Realist	Was born in northern Italy. Studied under Abelard. Became bishop of Paris. His *Sentences* became first standard medieval systematic theology. Emphasized seven sacraments.
HUGH OF ST. VICTOR	c.1096–1141	Saxony Paris	Summa Sententiarum	Faith is a certainty "above opinion and below science."	Mystic	Was born in Saxony. Entered school of St. Victor in Paris, where he later became master.

26. The Theology of Scholasticism (continued)

NAME	DATES	PLACES OF MINISTRY	REPRESENTATIVE WORKS	VIEW OF RELATIONSHIP OF FAITH AND REASON	VIEW OF NATURE OF UNIVERSALS	NOTABLE FACTS
ALBERTUS MAGNUS	c.1200– 1280	Bavaria Padua Paris Cologne	System of Nature The Praise of Mary	"Theology is science in the truest sense."	Moderate Realist	Was born in Bavaria. Entered Dominican order. Was teacher of Aquinas. Became bishop of Regensburg. Was renowned student of natural sciences. Was knowledgeable in Aristotelian philosophy. Advanced veneration of Mary.
JOHN BONAVEN- TURE	c.1217– 1274	Italy	On the Poverty of Christ Life of St. Francis Breviloquium Journey to the Mind of God	True knowledge comes only from the con- templation of the di- vine mystery.	Mystic	Was born in Tuscany. Entered Franciscan order at age 17. Became head of Franciscans. Advanced veneration of Mary. Was noted hymn-writer.
THOMAS AQUINAS	c.1225– 1274	Italy Paris Cologne	Summa Theologica Summa Contra Gentiles Contra Errores Graecorum	Natural reason leads one to the "vestibule of faith."	Moderate Realist	Was born to noble family in Aquino. Entered monastery at Monte Cassino at age 5. Entered Dominican order at age 19. Studied under Albertus Magnus. Taught at Paris, Cologne, and throughout Italy. Leaned heavily on writings of Aristotle and Augustine.
JOHN DUNS SCOTUS	c.1266– 1308	Britain Paris Cologne	Opus Oxoniense Questiones Quodlibetales	Knowledge of God can- not come from reason but must be accepted on the basis of the au- thority of the church. "A thing may at the same time be true in philosophy and false in theology."	Moderate Realist	Was born in British Isles. Entered Franciscan order. Studied and taught at Oxford. Earned doctorate in Paris. Was opponent of Aquinas. Influenced doctrine of Immaculate Conception. Protestants later coined the word "dunce" in reference to him.
WILLIAM OF OCKHAM	c.1280– 1349	England Paris Munich	Summa Logicae Dialogus Inter Magistrum et Discipulum	"Doctrines peculiar to revealed theology are not susceptible to proof by pure reason."	Nominalist— universalia post rem	Was born in Surrey. Entered Franciscan order. Studied under Duns Scotus. Taught in Paris. Was excommunicated for his views. Opposed papal infallibility. Denied civil authority of church.

27. Major Monastic Orders

CLASSIFI- CATION	ORDER	FOUNDER(S)	DATE	PLACE OF ORIGIN	SIGNIFICANT MEMBERS	NOTABLE FACTS
MILITARY ORDERS	BENEDICTINES	Benedict of Nursia	529	Monte Cassino, Italy	Bede Boniface	Became first monastic order. Order was based on Benedictine rule.
	KNIGHTS OF ST. JOHN (Hospitallers)	Raymund De Puy	1113	Jerusalem		Sought to care for pilgrims and later to fight in Crusades. In 1530 became Knights of Malta. Suppressed in 1798 by Napoleon. Were reestablished 1834.
	KNIGHTS TEMPLAR	Hugo De Payens Godfrey St. Omer	1119	Jerusalem		Sought to defend pilgrims by force. Became wealthy and powerful. Were suppressed 1312.
	TEUTONIC KNIGHTS	German Pilgrims	1190	Acre		Maintained hospitals in Holy Land. Did missionary work in Germany. Were suppressed 1523, but moved to and conquered East Prussia. Became ancestors of Junker landlords.
BENEDICTINES	CLUNIACS	William of Aquitane	910	Cluny, France	Gregory VII Urban II	Resulted from reform in Benedictine order. Followed Benedictine Rule.
	CISTERCIANS	Robert Molesme	1098	Citeaux, France	Eugene III Benedict XII Bernard of Clairvaux	Followed Benedictine Rule. Trappists are a branch of this order. Were suppressed 1790.
AUGUSTINIANS	AUGUSTINIANS				Thomas à Kempis Gerhard Groote Martin Luther Gregory of Rimini	Followed Rule of St. Augustine. Some were mendicants.
	PREMONSTRANTS	Norbert	1119	Premontre, France		Followed Rule of St. Augustine.

27. Major Monastic Orders (continued)

CLASSIFI-CATION	ORDER	FOUNDER(S)	DATE	PLACE OF ORIGIN	SIGNIFICANT MEMBERS	NOTABLE FACTS
INDEPENDENT	CARTHUSIANS	Bruno	c.1082	Chartreuse, France	Hugh of Lincoln	Followed Rule of the Carthusian Order. Were very strict; practiced self-flagellation.
INDEPENDENT	CARMELITES	Berthold	1156	Mt. Carmel	Theresa of Avila	Traced origins somewhat dubiously to Elijah. Later became mendicants.
MENDICANTS	DOMINICANS	Dominic Guzman	1216	Spain	Thomas Aquinas Albertus Magnus Johannes Eckhart John Tauler Bartolomeo De Las Casas Girolamo Savonarola Tomas De Torquemada	Used Rule of St. Augustine. Used by popes to root out heresy. Conducted Inquisition.
MENDICANTS	FRANCISCANS	Francis of Assisi	1223	Italy	Bonaventure Duns Scotus William of Ockham Roger Bacon Nicholas of Lyra	Their original rule was taken from Scripture. Took vow of absolute poverty. Produced Capuchins in 1525.
MENDICANTS	SOCIETY OF JESUS (Jesuits)	Ignatius Loyola	1540	Rome	Francis Xavier Robert De Nobili Matteo Ricci	Their rule was taken from Loyola's *Spiritual Exercises*. Were active in missions and education. Sought to eradicate Protestant Reformation. Were committed to absolute authority of pope. Were suppressed in 1773. Were restored in 1814.

28. Medieval Dissenters and Heretical Groups

GROUP	CHARACTERISTIC TEACHINGS	NOTABLE FACTS
PAULICIANS	dualistic docetic emphasized epistles of Paul similar to teachings of Marcion Old Testament and epistles of Peter rejected all external religious exercises rejected extremely ascetic	Began in 7th century. Were restricted to Eastern church. Were persecuted by Eastern church. Declined in 12th century.
BOGOMILS	dualistic ascetic Sabellian view of Trinity rejected sacraments	Were outgrowth of Euchites. Became prominent in Eastern Europe.
CATHARI (Patarenes, Albigensians)	dualistic docetic rejected sacraments extremely ascetic; opposed marriage similar to Manichaeans believed themselves the only true church divided into Perfect (only ones saved) and Believers believed in reincarnation rejected purgatory, indulgences often practiced suicide by starvation pacifistic	Began early 11th century. Were outgrowth of Paulicians and Bogomils. Followers were burned at stake throughout Europe. Their greatest strength was in southern France. Were targets of the Inquisition and several crusades.

28. Medieval Dissenters and Heretical Groups (continued)

GROUP	CHARACTERISTIC TEACHINGS	NOTABLE FACTS
WALDENSIANS	simple communal lifestyle preached Scripture in vernacular emphasized Sermon on the Mount encouraged lay preaching permitted women preachers denied purgatory	Were founded by Peter Waldo (d. c.1215). Began in southern France. Were also called Poor Men of Lyons. Were anathematized for preaching without church's consent. Were persecuted in northern Italy, Austria. Accepted Reformation in 1532.
LOLLARDS	encouraged lay preachers denied transubstantiation encouraged use of Bible in English pacifistic condemned pilgrimages, auricular confession, veneration of images denied purgatory, priestly celibacy	Were followers of John Wycliffe. Some were martyred, but many recanted when put on trial.
HUSSITES	emphasized authority of Scripture over church demanded partaking of cup by laity denied transubstantiation, veneration of saints, indulgences, auricular confession read Scripture in vernacular	Were followers of John Huss. Later became known as Unitas Fratrum or Bohemian Brethren. Five crusades were directed against them. Council of Basel made compromise settlement with Hussites. Were influenced by Waldensians. Are perpetuated today in form of Moravian church.

29. The Great Schism of the Papacy (1378–1417)

DATE	ROMAN POPES	AVIGNON POPES	CONCILIAR POPES
—1375—		GREGORY XI (1370–1378) Died in 1378, setting stage for Schism.	
—1378—			
—1381—	URBAN VI (1378–89) Ended "Babylonian Captivity" but caused Schism by alienating French cardinals.	CLEMENT VII (1378–94) After 3 years of warfare with supporters of Urban VI, moved to Avignon in 1381.	
—1384—			
—1387—			
—1390—	BONIFACE IX (1389–1404)		
—1393—			
—1396—		BENEDICT XIII (1394–1417) Deposed by Council of Pisa in 1409, but refused to step down; deposed by Council of Constance in 1417; returned to Spain, convinced to his dying day that he was the true pope.	
—1399—			
—1402—			
—1405—	INNOCENT VII (1404–06)		
—1408—	GREGORY XII (1406–15) Deposed by Council of Pisa in 1409, but refused to step down; deposed by Council of Constance in 1415.		ALEXANDER V (1409–10) Appointed by Council of Pisa.
—1411—			JOHN XXIII (1410–15) Deposed by Council of Constance in 1415.
—1414—			
—1417—			MARTIN V (1417–31) Named by Council of Constance to end Schism.
—1420—			
—1423—			

30. Medieval Ecumenical Councils

COUNCIL	DATE	KEY PARTICIPANTS	RESULTS
LATERAN I	1123	Callistus II	Confirmed Concordat of Worms. Forbade marriage of priests. Granted indulgences to crusaders.
LATERAN II	1139	Innocent II	Anathematized followers of antipope Anacletus II. Condemned schismatic groups. Confirmed decisions of Lateran I.
LATERAN III	1179	Alexander III	Condemned Cathari. Required two-thirds vote of cardinals for papal elections.
LATERAN IV	1215	Innocent III	Established Inquisition. Confirmed election of Emperor Frederick II. Denounced Magna Carta. Defined doctrine of transubstantiation. Confirmed Franciscans. Condemned Cathari and Waldensians. Prepared for Fifth Crusade.
LYONS I	1245	Innocent IV	Deposed Emperor Frederick II. Mourned loss of Jerusalem to Saracens.
LYONS II	1274	Gregory X	Reaffirmed *filioque* clause. Prohibited new monastic orders. Attempted to reunite Eastern and Western churches. Decided that cardinals were to receive no salary during papal elections.
VIENNE	1311–1312	Clement V	Suppressed Knights Templar. Attempted to encourage new crusade but failed. Condemned Beguines and Beghards.
PISA	1409	Peter D'Ailly Peter Philargi Guy De Maillesec	Asserted conciliar authority over papacy. Deposed Gregory XII (Rome) and Benedict XIII (Avignon) and elected Alexander V. Lacked power to enforce its decisions, left church with three rival popes.
CONSTANCE	1414–1418	John XXIII Sigismund Peter D'Ailly John Gerson	Ended papal schism by deposing all three claimants and appointing Martin V. Tried and executed John Huss. Affirmed authority of councils over church and insisted they be called as often as necessary.
BASEL	1431–1449	Martin V Eugene IV Julian Cesarini Nicholas of Cusa	Affirmed authority of council after Pope tried to disband it. Pope used disunity of council to reassert his authority. Reached compromise settlement with Hussites.

31. Forerunners of the Reformation

NAME	DATES	CHALLENGES TO THE CHURCH			PERSONAL DETAILS
		DOCTRINE	PRACTICE	AUTHORITY	
THOMAS BRADWARDINE	c.1290–1349	Emphasized grace of God in salvation.			Was an English theologian and mathematician. Was named Archbishop of Canterbury (1349). Died of Black Plague.
GREGORY OF RIMINI	d. 1358	Emphasized grace of God in salvation.			Was an Italian philosopher. Became an Augustinian monk.
JOHN WYCLIFFE	c.1329–1384	Denied transubstantiation.	Opposed church's accumulation of wealth, sale of indulgences.	Emphasized authority of Scripture.	Was professor of Oxford University. Was forced into retirement as a result of Peasants' Revolt (1381). Translated most of Vulgate into English. His body was exhumed and burned in 1428.
JOHN HUSS	c.1373–1415	Defined church by Christlike living rather than by sacraments.	Opposed sale of indulgences, veneration of images.	Emphasized authority of Scripture.	Was a Bohemian priest. Became professor at University of Prague. Was burned at stake by order of Council of Constance.
JOHN OF WESSEL	c.1420–1489	Denied transubstantiation.	Opposed sale of indulgences, priestly celibacy.	Emphasized authority of Scripture.	Was a German theologian. Was a member of Brethren of the Common Life. Died in prison after being convicted of heresy and after recanting.
GIROLAMO SAVONAROLA	1452–1498		Preached against papal immorality.		Was an Italian Dominican monk. Was hanged and burned for heresy in Florence.
DESIDERIUS ERASMUS	c.1466–1536		Attacked inconsistency and hypocrisy in the church.		Was a Dutch humanist. Compiled Greek text of New Testament used by Luther. In Praise of Folly mercilessly satirized failings of church.

32. Four Major Reformers

	MARTIN LUTHER	ULRICH ZWINGLI	JOHN CALVIN	JOHN KNOX
DATES	1483–1546	1484–1531	1509–1564	c.1514–1572
BIRTHPLACE	Eisleben, Germany	Upper Toggenburg, Switzerland	Noyon, France	Haddington, Scotland
EDUCATION	Leipzig	Vienna, Basel	Paris, Orleans	St. Andrews
ENTERED PRIESTHOOD	1507	1506		1536
REPRESENTATIVE WRITINGS	Ninety-five Theses On the Papacy at Rome Address to the German nobility The Babylonian Captivity of the Church The Bondage of the Will Larger Catechism Smaller Catechism Lectures on Romans Lectures on Galatians Table Talk	Concerning Freedom and Choice of Food Sixty-seven Conclusions	Institutes of the Christian Religion Commentaries on 49 books of Scripture	The First Blast of the Trumpet Against the Monstrous Regiment of Women History of the Reformation of Religion Within the Realm of Scotland
NOTABLE FACTS	Was influenced by Brethren of the Common Life. In 1505 entered Augustinian monastery. In 1508 began teaching at University of Wittenberg. In 1517 posted Ninety-five Theses. In 1520 was excommunicated. In 1521 was called to Diet of Worms. In 1521–34 translated Bible into German. In 1525 opposed Peasants' Revolt. In 1525 married Katherine von Bora.	Was influenced by Erasmus. Entered priesthood as respectable career. Opposed sale of mercenaries by Swiss. In 1518 was called to Zurich. His reformation went far beyond that of Luther. Some followers broke away to form Anabaptists, whom he persecuted. Was killed in battle against Catholic cantons.	Turned to Protestantism while studying in Paris. In 1533 was forced to flee Paris. In 1536 was persuaded by Farel to help in reforming Geneva. Was forced out of Geneva, settled in Strasbourg, where he married. In 1541 returned to Geneva, led Reformation there. Protestant refugees from all over Europe came to Geneva, took Calvin's ideas with them.	Was influenced by Thomas Gwilliam, George Wishart. Spent 1½ years as a galley slave. In 1549 went to England, preached against Catholicism. In 1553 went to Geneva, influenced by Calvin. In 1558 published The First Blast just as Elizabeth ascended throne. In 1559 returned to Scotland, led Reformation there.

33. Other German Reformers

NAME	DATES	EDUCATION	NOTABLE FACTS
THOMAS MÜNZER	c.1490–1525	Leipzig	Was influenced by Luther early in life. Became leader in Radical Reformation. Was associated with Zwickau prophets. Led Peasants' Revolt, was executed as a result. Bitterly hated Luther for condemning Peasants' Revolt.
ANDREAS VON CARLSTADT	c.1480–1541	Erfurt Cologne	Was colleague of Luther at Wittenberg. Defended Ninety-five Theses in debate against Johann Eck. Condemned with Luther in papal bull. Broke with Luther, influenced Swiss Anabaptists.
PHILIPP MELANCHTHON	1497–1560	Heidelberg Tübingen	Was influenced by Erasmus. Became professor of Greek at Wittenberg at age 21. Systematized and defended Luther's theology. Wrote first Protestant systematic theology–*Loci Communes.* Became known for attempts at reconciliation with Reformed and Catholics.
MATTHIAS FLACIUS ILLYRICUS	1520–1575	Venice Wittenberg	Studied under Luther and Melanchthon. Became professor of Hebrew at Wittenberg. Broke with Melanchthon, whom he saw as a compromiser. Vehemently criticized all with whom he disagreed.
MARTIN CHEMNITZ	1522–1586	Wittenberg	Studied under Melanchthon. Taught philosophy at Wittenberg. Set up church order in Brunswick. Helped draft Formula of Concord.
ZACHARIAS URSINUS	1534–1583	Wittenberg	Visited Calvin at Geneva. Taught at Breslau, Heidelberg. With Caspar Olevianus wrote Heidelberg Catechism. Became leader in German Reformed church.
CASPAR OLEVIANUS	1536–1587	Paris Orleans Bourges Geneva	Was born in France. Studied under Calvin and Beza. Helped organize church in Heidelberg along Reformed lines. With Zacharias Ursinus wrote Heidelberg Catechism.

34. Other Swiss Reformers

NAME	DATES	EDUCATION	NOTABLE FACTS
JOHANN OECOLAMPADIUS	1482– 1531	Bologna Heidelberg	Was trained in law, theology. Became a noted philologist. Was influenced by Erasmus, Melanchthon, Luther. Took the lead in bringing Reformation to Basel. Took part in Marburg Colloquy. Was a close associate of Zwingli.
GUILLAUME FAREL	1489– 1565	Paris	Studied under Jacques Lefevre. Was expelled from France, became traveling evangelist in Switzerland. Was influential in bringing Bern and Geneva into Reformation. Convinced Calvin to work on reforming church in Geneva. Spent latter part of life in Neuchatel.
MARTIN BUCER	1491– 1551	Heidelberg	Was called the Peacemaker of the Reformation. Was a Dominican monk. Erasmus influenced him in direction of humanism. After hearing Luther, he became Lutheran, left Dominicans. Led Reformation in Strasbourg, where he influenced Calvin. Often attempted to reconcile warring Lutherans, Reformed, and Catholics. Taught at Cambridge by special invitation from Thomas Cranmer.
HEINRICH BULLINGER	1504– 1575	Cologne	Was influenced by Erasmus, Luther, Melanchthon. Succeeded Zwingli at Zurich. Helped write First and Second Helvetic Confessions. Opposed presbyterianism.
THEODORE BEZA	1519– 1605	Orleans	Was trained in law. Turned to Protestantism in 1548 after severe illness. Taught Greek at Lausanne and Geneva. Headed academy in Geneva. Defended Reformed Protestantism at Colloquy of Poissy. Succeeded Calvin as religious leader of Geneva. Discovered Codex Bezae. Was advisor to French Huguenots.

35. The Radical Reformation

GROUP	CLASSIFICATION	KEY LEADERS	AREAS OF ACTIVITY	DISTINCTIVES
ANABAPTISTS	Biblical	Conrad Grebel Felix Manz Georg Blaurock Ludwig Hätzer Balthasar Hübmaier	Zurich and elsewhere in Switzerland and Holy Roman Empire	Repudiated church-state ties. Church considered voluntary association of committed believers.
HUTTERITES	Communal	Jacob Hutter	Moravia, later Dakotas and Western Canada	Repudiated infant baptism. Practiced strict church discipline. Were pacifists. Some practiced community of goods. Had religious toleration for all.
SCHWENK-FELDERS	Mystical	Caspar Schwenkfeld Von Ossig	Germany, later Pennsylvania	Maintained simplicity of dress and lifestyle. Some followed Michael Sattler's *Schleitheim Confession*. Some had mystical tendencies.
MENNONITES	Biblical	Menno Simons	Netherlands, later Pennsylvania and elsewhere	
AMISH	Biblical	Jacob Ammann	Switzerland, later Pennsylvania and elsewhere	

36. The English Reformers

NAME	DATES	EDUCATION	NOTABLE FACTS
WILLIAM TYNDALE	c.1494– 1536	Oxford Cambridge	Was forced into exile, published translation of New Testament in English while in hiding on Continent. Was hounded all over Europe by his enemies. Was arrested and executed in Brussels.
THOMAS CROMWELL	c.1485– 1540	Unknown	Was assistant to Cardinal Wolsey. Became a member of Parliament. Held office of vicar-general under Henry VIII. Supervised dissolution of monasteries. Encouraged translation and publication of Great Bible. Attempted to arrange a marriage alliance between Henry VIII and German Lutherans. Was beheaded for treason.
THOMAS CRANMER	1489– 1556	Cambridge	Supported Henry VIII in effort to divorce Catherine of Aragon. In 1533 was named Archbishop of Canterbury. Introduced moderate reforms under Henry VIII and Edward VI. Worked on production of first and second Book of Common Prayer. Was arrested and convicted of treason and heresy under Mary Tudor. Recanted under duress; burned at stake while denying his recantation.
HUGH LATIMER	c.1485– 1555	Cambridge	In 1535 became bishop of Worcester. Was twice imprisoned by Henry VIII. Became leading preacher during reign of Edward VI. Was burned at stake at Oxford under Mary Tudor.
NICHOLAS RIDLEY	c.1500– 1555	Cambridge	Was chaplain to Cranmer, later to Henry VIII. In 1547 was named bishop of Rochester. In 1550 was named bishop of London. Helped produce first and second Book of Common Prayer. Was arrested and burned at stake with Latimer.
JOHN HOOPER	c.1495– 1555	Oxford	Entered Augustinian monastery. Was converted to Protestantism, forced to flee country. Became friend of Bullinger while in Zurich. Became bishop of Gloucester and Worcester. Was burned at stake under Mary Tudor.
MILES COVERDALE	1488– 1568	Cambridge	Entered Augustinian monastery. Left monastery when converted to Protestantism; was forced to flee country. Assisted Tyndale in his translation work. Completed Tyndale's translation after Tyndale's death. Worked on Great Bible and Geneva Bible. In 1551 was named bishop of Exeter. Was exiled under Mary Tudor.
MATTHEW PARKER	1504– 1575	Cambridge	Was chaplain to Anne Boleyn. Was a friend of Bucer when latter was in England. Was forced into hiding under Mary Tudor. In 1559 reluctantly accepted appointment as Archbishop of Canterbury. Worked on Elizabeth Settlement. Opposed Puritans.

37. The English Puritans

NAME	DATES	EDUCATION	ECCLESIASTICAL AFFILIATION	REPRESENTATIVE WRITINGS	NOTABLE FACTS
THOMAS CARTWRIGHT	1535–1603	Cambridge	Presbyterian	Holy Discipline	Lost teaching post at Cambridge for advocating presbyterianism. Spent time in Geneva. Was imprisoned several times for defense of Puritanism.
HENRY JACOB	1563–1624	Oxford	Congregational		Was part of Brownist movement. Became a member of John Robinson's church in Leyden. Founded first permanent Congregational church in England at Southwark.
OLIVER CROMWELL	1599–1658	Cambridge	Congregational		Was a member of Parliament from 1628. Led Parliamentary army during Civil War. Became Lord Protector of England after execution of Charles I. Refused proffered crown in 1656.
THOMAS GOODWIN	1600–1679	Cambridge	Congregational	Sermon collections	Became a Separatist through influence of John Cotton. Moved to Holland after harassment by Archbishop Laud. Led Congregationalists at Westminster Assembly. Became an advisor to Cromwell.
JOHN MILTON	1608–1674	Cambridge	Congregational	Areopagitica Paradise Lost	Was a Puritan poet and pamphleteer. Decided against Anglican ministry because of Archbishop Laud. Was in government service under Cromwell. Was forced into retirement by Restoration.
RICHARD BAXTER	1615–1691		Anglican	The Saints' Everlasting Rest The Reformed Pastor A Call to the Unconverted	Took mediating position in political and theological disputes of his day. Briefly served as chaplain to Charles II.

37. The English Puritans (continued)

NAME	DATES	EDUCATION	ECCLESIASTICAL AFFILIATION	REPRESENTATIVE WRITINGS	NOTABLE FACTS
JOHN OWEN	1616–1683	Oxford	Congregational	The Epistle to the Hebrews	Entered Oxford at age 12; received master's degree at age 19. Supported Parliamentary cause in Civil War. Served as chaplain to Cromwell. Became vice-chancellor at Oxford.
JOHN BUNYAN	1628–1688		Baptist	Pilgrim's Progress The Holy War Grace Abounding to the Chief of Sinners	Was a tinker by trade. Fought in Parliamentary army. Became a Baptist preacher in Bedford. Was imprisoned for twelve years after Restoration.
JOHN FLAVEL	c.1630–1691	Oxford	Presbyterian	Treatise on the Soul The Methods of Grace	Was a pastor at Dartmouth until forced out by Clarendon Code. Returned to pastorate in 1671.
JOHN HOWE	1630–1706	Cambridge Oxford	Anglican	Blessedness of the Righteous	For many years was pastor at Great Torrington. Became a chaplain to Oliver and later to Richard Cromwell. Was among more irenic of Puritans.
JOSEPH ALLEINE	1634–1668	Oxford	Presbyterian	An Alarm to the Unconverted	Was imprisoned in 1663 for singing psalms and preaching to his family in his own home.
MATTHEW HENRY	1662–1714	By father at home	Presbyterian	Matthew Henry's Commentary	Originally studied law. Served as pastor at Chester, 1687–1712. Wrote six-volume devotional commentary still widely used.

38. Leaders of the Catholic Counterreformation

NAME	DATES	HOME COUNTRY	EDUCATION	NOTABLE FACTS
TOMAS DE TORQUEMADA	1420–1498	Spain	Valladolid	Became a Dominican monk. Was confessor of Ferdinand and Isabella. Was first Inquisitor-General of Spain. Was active in driving Jews and Moors from Spain.
FRANCISCO JIMENES	1436–1517	Spain	Salamanca	Was a prominent Spanish preacher. Entered Franciscan order. Was confessor of Queen Isabella. Became archbishop of Toledo, later cardinal. Founded University of Alcala. Oversaw printing of Complutensian Polyglot.
GIOVANNI CARAFFA (Paul IV)	1476–1559	Italy	Naples	Became bishop of Chiete in 1506. Was papal envoy to England, Flanders, Spain. Helped found Theatines in 1524. Was made cardinal in 1536. Was pope from 1555. Initiated *Index of Prohibited Books*.
JACOPO SADOLETO	1477–1547	Italy	Pisa Ferraro Rome	Served as secretary to Leo X and Clement VII. Became cardinal with other reformers in 1536. Corresponded with Melanchthon and Calvin, attempting to reconcile them to Catholic Church. His reform ideas were largely ignored by hierarchy.
GASPARO CONTARINI	1483–1542	Italy	Padua	Was appointed ambassador of Venice to England, Spain, Italy. Became cardinal in 1536. Attempted reconciliation with Protestants. Produced joint statement on justification with Melanchthon and Bucer at Regensburg in 1541.
IGNATIUS LOYOLA	1491–1556	Spain	Alcala Salamanca Paris	Was soldier, wounded and lamed in 1521. Entered Dominican order. Wrote *Spiritual Exercises*. Founded Society of Jesus in 1534. Founded Roman College in 1551.

38. Leaders of the Catholic Counterreformation (continued)

NAME	DATES	HOME COUNTRY	EDUCATION	NOTABLE FACTS
REGINALD POLE	1500–1558	England	Oxford Padua	Was exiled for opposition to Henry VIII's divorce. Became cardinal in 1536. Attempted to restore England to Catholicism. Succeeded Cranmer as archbishop of Canterbury.
MICHELE GHISLIERI (Pius V)	1504–1572	Italy	Bosco	Entered Dominican order. Headed Roman Inquisition. Became cardinal in 1557, pope in 1566. Encouraged destruction of Protestants in Netherlands and France. Excommunicated Elizabeth I of England.
JAMES LAYNEZ	1512–1565	Spain	Alcala Paris	Was one of six original members of Society of Jesus. Preached forcefully against Protestantism. Later became head of Jesuits. Led papal party at Council of Trent, helped shape anti-Protestant canons.
PETER CANISIUS	1521–1597	Germany	Cologne	Entered Society of Jesus in 1543. Was a leader of Counterreformation in southern Germany. Wrote three catechisms, which were translated into 12 languages and widely disseminated.
CHARLES BORROMEO	1538–1584	Italy	Arona	Was named abbot of Arona monastery at age 12. Became cardinal in 1559, archbishop of Milan in 1560. Was an active reforming influence at Council of Trent. Founded many schools and orphanages.
ROBERT BELLARMINE	1542–1621	Italy	Padua Louvain	Entered Society of Jesus in 1560. Became professor of theology at Louvain. Was the chief Catholic apologist of his age. Became cardinal in 1599. Opposed teachings of Galileo.

39. Leaders of the French Huguenots

NAME	DATES	ROLE IN MOVEMENT	NOTABLE FACTS
GASPARD DE COLIGNY	1519–1572	Military Leader	Was born into noble family. Became admiral of France in 1552. Became Protestant while in Spanish prison in Netherlands. Was adviser to Charles IX. Established Huguenot colonies in Brazil and Florida. Was murdered in St. Bartholomew's Day Massacre.
ANNE DU BOURG	c.1520–1559	Martyr	Was trained in law. Taught at University of Orleans. Became outspoken advocate of Protestantism in 1559. Was condemned for heresy, strangled, and burned.
PHILIPPE DUPLESSIS-MORNAY	1549–1623	Statesman	Was adviser to Henry of Navarre. Was appointed ambassador to England and the Netherlands. Served as governor of Saumur. Founded University of Saumur. Wrote in defense of Reformed faith.
HENRY IV	1553–1610	Military Leader	Was born into Huguenot Bourbon family of Navarre. Married Catholic Margaret of Valois in 1572. Led Huguenots after death of Coligny. Became first Bourbon king of France after converting to Catholicism, saying, "Paris is worth a mass." Issued Edict of Nantes in 1598 granting toleration to Huguenots. Was assassinated by Catholic fanatic in 1610.
PIERRE DU MOULIN	1568–1658	Pastor	Studied at Cambridge University. Taught at University of Leyden. Pastored Reformed church at Charenton for many years.
JEAN DAILLÉ	1594–1670	Theologian	Was educated at Saumur. Became chaplain to Duplessis-Mornay. Attacked authority of patristic writings. Supported Amyraldianism.
MOSES AMYRAUT	1596–1664	Theologian	Studied under Scotsman John Cameron at Saumur. Became professor at University of Saumur. Attempted compromise between Calvinism and Arminianism; it became known as Amyraldianism.
PIERRE JURIEU	1637–1713	Theologian	Studied at Saumur. Defended Reformed faith against critics. Believed Apocalypse predicted restoration of Huguenots. Advocated violent overthrow of Louis XIV. Was viewed as a prophet by Camisards in War of the Cevennes.
ANTOINE COURT	1696–1760	Pastor	Led Church of the Desert during persecution of Louis XIV. Established seminary to train Huguenot ministers in Lausanne and operated it for 30 years. Carried on voluminous correspondence with Reformed leaders.
PAUL RABAUT	1718–1794	Pastor	Studied under Court at Lausanne. Ministered in hiding to Church of the Desert. Became recognized as leader of Reformed Protestants in France. Was instrumental in gaining eventual recognition for Protestants.

40. Religious Wars of the Reformation

WAR	DATES	LOCALITY	MAJOR PARTICIPANTS	KEY LEADERS	OUTCOME
PEASANTS' REVOLT	1524– 1525	Germany	Peasants vs. Nobility	Thomas Münzer Philip of Hesse	Brutal suppression of peasants Twelve Articles
KAPPEL WARS	1529, 1531	Switzerland	Catholic vs. Protestant cantons	Ulrich Zwingli	Death of Zwingli and defeat of Protestants
SMALCALD WAR	1546– 1555	Germany	German Protestants vs. Holy Roman Empire	Emperor Charles V Philip of Hesse John Frederick of Saxony Duke Maurice of Saxony	Defeat of Protestants Settlement of Interim Renewed hostilities Legal recognition of Lutherans Peace of Augsburg *Cuius Regio, Eius Religio*
DUTCH REVOLT	1559– 1579	Netherlands	Spain vs. Netherlands	Philip II William the Silent	Netherlands divided by Protestant Union of Utrecht in north (Holland), Catholic League of Arras in south (Belgium)
THIRTY YEARS' WAR	1618– 1648	Germany and Central Europe	Holy Roman Empire Germany Denmark Sweden France Spain	Elector Palatine Frederick V Emperor Ferdinand Gustavus Adolphus Duke Maximilian of Bavaria Johan Tilly Christian IV Albrecht Wallenstein	Peace of Westphalia Political and religious boundaries fixed Limited religious toleration approved Jesuits excluded from Protestant lands Calvinism recognized

41. Theological Issues—Protestant vs. Catholic

AREA	ISSUE	PROTESTANT POSITION	CATHOLIC POSITION
SCRIPTURE	SUFFICIENCY	*Sola Scriptura*	tradition of equal authority with Scripture
	APOCRYPHA	rejected	accepted
ANTHRO-POLOGY	ORIGINAL SIN	total depravity and guilt inherited from Adam	corruption and predisposition to evil inherited from Adam
	HUMAN WILL	in bondage to sin	free to do spiritual good
SOTERIOLOGY	PREDESTINATION	rooted in God's decrees	rooted in God's foreknowledge
	ATONEMENT	Christ's death a substitutionary penal sacrifice	Christ's death the merit for blessings of salvation—blessings passed on to sinners through sacraments
	GRACE OF GOD	common grace given to all; saving grace given to elect	prevenient grace, given at baptism, enabling one to believe; efficacious grace cooperating with the will, enabling one to obey
	GOOD WORKS	produced by the grace of God, unworthy of merit of any kind	meritorious
	REGENERATION	work of the Holy Spirit in the elect	grace infused at baptism
	JUSTIFICATION	objective, final, judicial act of God	forgiveness of sins received at baptism, may be lost by committing mortal sin, regained by penance
ECCLESIOLOGY	CHURCH AND SALVATION	distinction between visible and invisible church	outside the (visible) church there is no salvation
	SACRAMENTS	means of grace only as received by faith	convey justifying and sanctifying grace *ex opere operato*
	PRIESTHOOD	all believers priests	mediators between God and man
	TRANSUBSTANTIATION	rejected	affirmed
ESCHA-TOLOGY	PURGATORY	denied	affirmed

42. Theological Issues—Lutheran vs. Reformed

ISSUE	LUTHERAN POSITION	REFORMED POSITION
ORDO SALUTIS	calling, illumination, conversion, regeneration, justification, sanctification, glorification	election, predestination, union with Christ, calling, regeneration, faith, repentance, justification, sanctification, glorification
GRACE OF GOD	grace received through baptism or preaching, enabling one to avoid resisting the regenerating grace of God	irresistible
REPENTANCE	leads to faith	flows from faith
BAPTISM	works regeneration, removing guilt and power of sin	incorporation into the Covenant of Grace
LORD'S SUPPER	Christ present in the sacrament objectively	sign and seal of the Covenant of Grace to believers; Christ present by faith
CHURCH AND STATE	state church to tutor in the faith the rulers who support Protestantism	Holy Commonwealth, in which church and state both Christian yet perform their separate functions
REGULATIVE PRINCIPLE	Whatever is not forbidden in Scripture is permissible.	Whatever is not commanded in Scripture is forbidden.

43. Theological Issues—Calvinist vs. Arminian

ISSUE	CALVINIST POSITION	ARMINIAN POSITION
ORIGINAL SIN	total depravity and guilt inherited from Adam	weakness inherited from Adam
HUMAN WILL	in bondage to sin	free to do spiritual good
GRACE OF GOD	common grace given to all; saving grace given to elect	enabling grace given to all; saving grace given to those who believe; persevering grace given to those who obey
PREDESTINATION	rooted in God's decrees	rooted in God's fore-knowledge
REGENERATION	monergistic	synergistic
ATONEMENT	Christ's death a substitutionary penal sacrifice	Christ's death a sacrifice that God benevolently accepted in place of a penalty
EXTENT OF ATONEMENT	intended only for the elect	intended for all
APPLICATION OF ATONE-MENT	by power of the Holy Spirit according to the will of God	by power of the Holy Spirit in response to the will of the sinner
ORDO SALUTIS	election, predestination, union with Christ, calling, regeneration, faith, repentance, justification, sanctification, glorification	calling, faith, repentance, regeneration, justification, perseverance, glorification
PERSEVERANCE	perseverance of all the elect by the grace of God	perseverance dependent on obedience

44. A Family Tree of Protestant Denominational Groups

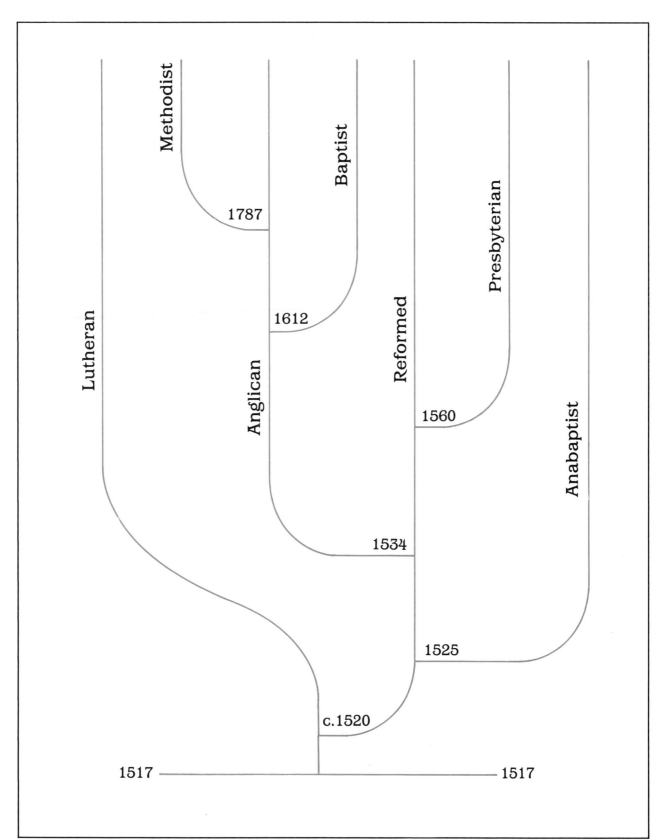

45. English Deism and Its Opponents

	NAME	DATES	REPRESENTATIVE WRITINGS	CONTRIBUTIONS TO DEBATE
FORERUNNERS OF DEISM	THOMAS HOBBES	1588–1679	Leviathan Behemoth	All knowledge derived from senses and reason. Scripture is not contrary to reason. Existence attributed to material only.
	JOHN LOCKE	1632–1704	The Reasonableness of Christianity Essay Concerning Human Understanding	Revelation cannot contradict reason. Taught the idea of a tabula rasa. Knowledge comes by reflection on sensations.
	ISAAC NEWTON	1642–1727	Principia Mathematica	His picture of a mechanistic universe was eagerly seized by Deists.
LEADING DEISTS	EDWARD HERBERT, LORD CHERBURY	1583–1648	De Veritate	Was influenced by Montaigne. Supernatural revelation is not necessary for religion.
	JOHN TOLAND	1670–1722	Christianity Not Mysterious	Denied that Christianity introduced anything not previously known.
	ANTHONY COLLINS	1676–1729	A Discourse of Free Thinking Discourse on the Grounds and Reasons of the Christian Religion	Since biblical writers were freethinkers, so should we be. There is no real correspondence between Old Testament prophecies and the life of Christ.
	MATTHEW TINDAL	1655–1733	Christianity as Old as the Creation	Asserted absolute sufficiency of natural religion. Taught that Christianity is to be tested by natural religion. Declared that creation is perfect, so nothing can or should be added to it.
	THOMAS WOOLSTON	1669–1733	Six Discourses on the Miracles of Our Saviour	Insisted that New Testament miracles were symbolic, not factual. Affirmed that Resurrection was not a hoax perpetrated by disciples.

45. English Deism and Its Opponents (continued)

	NAME	DATES	REPRESENTATIVE WRITINGS	CONTRIBUTIONS TO DEBATE
APOLOGISTS AGAINST DEISM	GEORGE BERKELEY	1685–1753	Alciphron	Attributed a real existence to God's ideas, not to matter.
	WILLIAM LAW	1686–1761	The Case of Reason	Attempted to refute Tindal's arguments. Declared that God's actions are not always according to human reason. His devotional works strongly influenced John Wesley.
	JOSEPH BUTLER	1692–1752	Analogy of Religion	Was greatest opponent of Deism. His *Analogy* was used as an Apologetics text for 200 years. Taught that natural religion is insufficient without complementary revelation. Said that probable truth of revealed religion is as strong as probable truth of natural religion.
	WILLIAM WARBURTON	1698–1779	The Divine Legation of Moses Principles of Natural and Revealed Religion	Attempted to demonstrate divine origin of the Old Testament on basis of its lack of teaching on afterlife.
	WILLIAM PALEY	1743–1805	View of the Evidences of Christianity Natural Theology	Gave lucid expression to anti-Deist apologetic. Gave classical form of teleological argument for the existence of God.

46. German Pietism and English Methodism—
A Comparison

	PIETISM	METHODISM
FOUNDER	Philipp Jakob Spener (1635–1705)	John Wesley (1703–1791)
RELIGIOUS SITUATION	Stagnant Orthodoxy of Post-Reformation Scholastic Lutheranism	Rationalistic Deism of Post-Puritan Anglicanism
FOUNDATIONAL BOOK	Spener, *Pia Desideria*	William Law, *A Serious Call to a Devout and Holy Life*
EDUCATIONAL CENTER	University of Halle	Oxford University
ORGANIZATION	Conventicles	Methodist societies
OTHER KEY FIGURES	Auguste H. Francke (1663–1727) J. A. Bengel (1687–1752) Nikolaus Ludwig Von Zinzendorf (1700–1760) Peter Boehler (1712–1775) Alexander Mack (1679–1735)	Charles Wesley (1707–1788) George Whitefield (1714–1770) Thomas Coke (1747–1814) Francis Asbury (1745–1816) Selina Hastings, Countess of Huntingdon (1707–1791)
RESULTING CHURCHES	Church of the Brethren Moravian Church	Methodist Church Calvinistic Methodists (Countess of Huntingdon's Connexion)
COMMON EMPHASES	Practical holiness Personal Bible study Need for conscious conversion Evangelistic preaching Devotional exercises Relief of poor and needy Experience more than doctrine	
PIETIST INFLU-ENCES ON METHODISM	Wesleys met Moravians on ship to Georgia, were impressed with their quiet confidence (1735). Moravian Spangenberg questioned John Wesley in Georgia. John Wesley sought out Moravians in London; Boehler was instrumental in his conversion (1738). John Wesley visited Zinzendorf at Herrnhut (1738). Methodist societies were established, based on model of Pietist conventicles (1738).	

47. John Wesley and George Whitefield—A Contrast

	WESLEY	WHITEFIELD
PARENTAGE	Son of Anglican rector in Epworth	Son of tavern keeper in Gloucester
EARLY LIFE	Strict religious upbringing supervised by mother, Susanna	Raised surrounded by worldly influences by mother, Elizabeth, who was widowed when George was 2
CONVERSION	Aldersgate Street, London, at age 35	Oxford University, at age 21
ORDINATION	Church of England, 1728, at age 25	Church of England 1736, at age 22
PREACHING STYLE	Intellectual, doctrinal	Dramatic, emotional
DOCTRINE	Arminian (though closer to Pietist semi-Augustinianism than to Dutch Arminianism)	Calvinistic
ORGANIZATIONAL ABILITY	Was exceptional organizer; maintained personal control over total organization of Methodist societies.	Was able organizer, but preferred to preach and leave organizing to others.
MINISTRY OUTSIDE ENGLAND	Did early unsuccessful missionary work in Georgia. Later preached in Scotland and Ireland. Appointed bishops to supervise work in America.	Visited Scotland 14 times, participating in Cambuslang revival. Visited America 7 times, becoming catalyst of First Great Awakening.
LEGACY	Methodist Church	Calvinistic Methodists; influence on Evangelical Party in Church of England

48. Other European Revivals

LOCATION	TIME	LEADING REVIVALISTS	RESULTING ORGANIZATIONS
WALES	Mid-18th century	Howell Harris (1714–1773) Daniel Rowland (c.1713–1790) William Williams (1717–1791)	
	Early 19th century	Christmas Evans (1766–1838) John Elias (1774–1841)	Calvinistic Methodist Church of Wales
	Early 20th century	Evan Roberts (1878–1951)	
SCOTLAND	Early–mid-19th century	Robert Haldane (1764–1842) James Haldane (1768–1851) Thomas Chalmers (1780–1847) Robert Murray McCheyne (1814–1843)	Society for the Propagation of the Gospel at Home Free Church of Scotland
SWITZERLAND	Early–mid-19th century	Robert Haldane (1764–1842) Cesar Malan (1787–1864) François Gaussen (1790–1863) J. H. Merle D'Aubigné (1794–1872)	Evangelical Society of Geneva Evangelical Seminary in Geneva
FRANCE	Early–mid-19th century	Frederick Monod (1794–1863) Adolphe Monod (1802–1856)	Union of Evangelical Churches of France *Archives Du Christianisme*
NETHERLANDS	Late 19th century	Groen van Prinsterer (c.1800–1867) Abraham Kuyper (1837–1920)	Free Reformed Church of the Netherlands Free University of Amsterdam

49. Evangelical Social Reformers in England

NAME	DATES	AREAS OF SOCIAL CONCERN	NOTABLE FACTS
JOHN NEWTON	1725–1807	Abolition of slavery	Was a sailor on slave ship. Became Anglican minister. Wrote many hymns, including "Amazing Grace." Influenced Wilberforce against slavery.
JOHN HOWARD	1726–1790	Prison reform	Was imprisoned by pirates in Frances. Wrote *State of the Prisons*. His impact extended throughout Europe.
ROBERT RAIKES	1735–1811	Education of urban poor	Was a newspaper publisher. Popularized the Sunday school. Was encouraged by John Wesley.
GRANVILLE SHARP	1735–1813	Abolition of slavery	Was associated with Clapham sect. Stimulated founding of Sierra Leone. His work led to emancipation of slaves in England in 1772.
WILLIAM WILBERFORCE	1759–1833	Abolition of slavery	Was greatest British abolitionist. Became a member of Claphan sect. Served many years in Parliament. Helped found British and Foreign Bible Society and Church Missionary Society. His work led to abolition of slave trade and emancipation of slaves throughout British Empire.
A. A. COOPER, SEVENTH EARL OF SHAFTESBURY	1801–1885	Humane treatment of insane / Reform of labor laws	Served many years in Parliament. Headed Lunacy Commission. Promoted passage of female and child labor laws.
GEORGE MÜLLER	1805–1898	Care of orphans	Was a member of Plymouth Brethren. Founded faith orphanage in Bristol but never solicited contributions for it. Was influenced by Pietist A. H. Francke.
WILLIAM BOOTH	1829–1912	Urban poverty	Was a Methodist minister. Wrote *In Darkest England*. Founded Salvation Army.

50. Major Figures in German Liberal Theology

NAME	DATES	REPRESENTATIVE WRITINGS	NOTABLE FACTS
F. C. BAUR	1762–1860	Paul the Apostle of Jesus Christ	Taught at University of Tübingen. Applied Hegelian dialectic to New Testament, postulating Petrine and Pauline antitheses leading to Old Catholic synthesis. Denied authenticity of most of New Testament.
FRIEDRICH SCHLEIERMACHER	1768–1834	On Religion: Speeches to Its Cultured Despisers The Christian Faith	Was raised in Pietist family. Attended University of Halle, later taught there and at Berlin. Rooted religion in feeling of absolute dependence.
DAVID FRIEDRICH STRAUSS	1808–1874	Life of Jesus The Old and the New Faith	Studied under Baur at Tübingen. Radical ideas cost him his teaching career. Eventually abandoned Christianity for "religion of humanity."
ALBRECHT RITSCHL	1822–1889	The Christian Doctrine of Justification and Reconciliation Theology and Metaphysics	Studied under Baur at Tübingen. Taught at Bonn and Göttingen. Rejected metaphysics. Emphasized ethical and social dimensions of Christianity. Pioneered "theology of moral value."
JULIUS WELLHAUSEN	1844–1918	History of Israel	Studied and taught at Göttingen. Originated Documentary Hypothesis (JEDP).
ADOLF VON HARNACK	1851–1930	What Is Christianity? History of Dogma The Mission and Expansion of Christianity in the First Three Centuries	Was ancient church historian. Promulgated Social Gospel (fatherhood of God and brotherhood of man). Taught at University of Berlin.

50. Major Figures in German Liberal Theology (continued)

NAME	DATES	REPRESENTATIVE WRITINGS	NOTABLE FACTS
ALBERT SCHWEITZER	1875– 1965	The Quest of the Historical Jesus	Earned doctorates in theology, medicine, and music. Was a missionary to Africa. Received Nobel Peace Prize (1952). Taught that Jesus mistakenly believed the end of the world was near.
KARL BARTH	1886– 1968	Church Dogmatics Commentary on the Epistle to the Romans	Was a Swiss theologian, founder of Neoorthodoxy. Broke from traditional liberalism. Was the author of the Barmen Declaration. Was ousted from Germany for opposition to Hitler. His teachings included absolute transcendence of God, Bible's becoming the Word of God as it is read, and election of all people in Christ.
RUDOLF BULTMANN	1884– 1976	Kerygma and Myth Theology of the New Testament Jesus and the Word The Form of the Synoptic Tradition	Was an existentialist New Testament scholar. Was noted for "demythologizing" New Testament accounts. Taught at University of Marburg. Pioneered Form Criticism.
PAUL TILLICH	1886– 1965	Dynamics of Faith Systematic Theology The Courage to Be	Was existentialist theologian. Was forced out of Germany under Hitler. Taught at Union Seminary in New York, Columbia, Harvard, University of Chicago. Saw God as Ground of Being and faith as Ultimate Concern.
DIETRICH BONHOEFFER	1906– 1945	The Cost of Discipleship Letters and Papers From Prison	Studied under Harnack and Barth. Helped draft the Barmen Declaration. Was a leader in Confessing Church. Had mystical tendencies. Was executed in a Nazi concentration camp.

51. Modern Roman Catholic Ecumenical Councils

	COUNCIL OF TRENT	FIRST VATICAN COUNCIL	SECOND VATICAN COUNCIL
DATES	1545–1563	1869–1870	1962–1965
CALLED BY	Paul III	Pius IX	John XXIII
PAPAL BULL	*Laetare Hierusalem*	*Aeterni Patris*	*Humanae Salutis*
NUMBER AND DATES OF SESSIONS	3 sessions 1545–47; 1551–52; 1562–63	1 session 12/8/69–7/18/70	4 sessions 10/11–12/8/62; 9/29–12/4/63; 9/14–11/21/64; 9/14–12/8/65
KEY FIGURES	Paul III Julius III Pius IV James Laynez Giovanni Morone	Pius IX Henry Manning Karl J. Hefele Felix Dupanloup	John XXIII Paul VI Karl Rahner Hans Küng
CENTRAL FOCUS	Reform the church. Halt Protestant Reformation.	Papal infallibility	Aggiornamento—Updating the church
MAJOR DECISIONS	Tradition bears same authority as Scripture. Apocrypha was included in canon of Scripture. Vulgate was declared official Bible of the church. Protestant teachings on original sin and justification by faith alone were rejected. Number of sacraments were fixed at seven, giving grace *ex opere operato*. Transubstantiation was affirmed. Moral standards for clergy were reaffirmed. Index was greatly expanded by the addition of Protestant writings.	Promulgated dogma of papal infallibility when speaking *ex cathedra* on matters of faith and morals.	Protestants were referred to as "separated brethren." Dialogue with other faiths was encouraged. Translation and reading of Bible was encouraged. Mass was required to be in vernacular, with laity participating. Religious freedom for all was upheld. Excommunications of Great Schism of 1054 were revoked. Index was eliminated. Papal infallibility, tradition, Catholic church as only way of salvation were reaffirmed. Veneration of Mary was encouraged. Laity were recognized as spiritual priests. Collegiality of pope and bishops was recognized.

52. The Growth and Development of the World Council of Churches

INTERNATIONAL MISSIONARY COUNCIL	FAITH AND ORDER	LIFE AND WORK
1910—World Missionary Conference, Edinburgh, Scotland: "The Evangelization of the World in this Generation"		
1921—International Missionary Council formed at Lake Mohonk, New York, U.S.A.		
	1927—Faith and Order, Lausanne, Switzerland	1925—Life and Work, Stockholm, Sweden
1928—International Missionary Council, Jerusalem, Palestine		
	1937—Faith and Order, Edinburgh, Scotland	1937—Life and Work, Oxford, England
	1938—Joint Committee, Utrecht, Netherlands	
1947—International Missionary Council, Whitby, Canada		
	1948—World Council of Churches, Amsterdam, Netherlands: "Man's Disorder and God's Design"	
1952—International Missionary Council, Willingen, Netherlands: "The Missionary Obligation of the Church"	1952—Commission on Faith and Order, Lund, Sweden	
	1954—World Council of Churches, Evanston, Illinois, U.S.A.: "Christ, The Hope of the World"	
1958—International Missionary Council, Ghana		
1961—International Missionary Council joins World Council of Churches, New Delhi, India: "Jesus Christ, the Light of the World"		
1963—Commission on World Mission and Evangelism, Mexico City, Mexico: "Witness in Six Continents"	1963—Commission on Faith and Order, Montreal, Canada	
		1966—Department of Church and Society, Geneva, Switzerland: "Christians in the Technical and Social Revolutions of Our Time"
1968—World Council of Churches, Uppsala, Sweden: "Behold, I Make All Things New"		
1972—Commission on World Missions and Evangelism, Bangkok, Thailand: "Salvation Today"		
1975—World Council of Churches, Nairobi, Kenya		
1983—World Council of Churches, Vancouver, Canada: "Jesus Christ, The Life of the World"		

53. Religion in the Thirteen Colonies

COLONY	CHARTER DATE	CHARTER RECIPIENT	FIRST SETTLED	SETTLERS	MAIN REASON FOR COMING	RELIGIOUS ORIENTATION	ESTABLISHED CHURCH
VIRGINIA	1606	Virginia Company	1607	English	Economic gain	Anglican	Church of England
	1624	Royal Colony					
MASSACHUSETTS	1619	Pilgrims	1620	Pilgrims	Religious freedom	Separatists	Congregational
	1629	Mass. Bay Co.		Puritans	Establish theocracy	Congregationalist	
	1684	Royal Colony					
NEW HAMPSHIRE	1679	Royal Colony	1623	Puritans	Expansion from Massachusetts Bay	Congregationalist	Congregational
NEW YORK	1664	Royal Colony	1624	Dutch	Economic gain	Dutch Reformed	Church of England (1692)
MARYLAND	1632	Lord Baltimore	1634	English	Refuge for Roman Catholics	Roman Catholic and other	Church of England (1691)
	1691	Royal Colony					
CONNECTICUT	1662	John Winthrop, Jr. (Royal Colony)	1634	Puritans	Expansion from Massachusetts Bay	Congregationalist	Congregational
RHODE ISLAND	1644	Roger Williams	1636	English	Radicals fleeing Massachusetts Bay	Congregationalist	None
	1663	Renewed					
NEW JERSEY	1664	John Berkeley George Carteret	1638	Swedish	Economic gain	Lutheran	None
	1702	Royal Colony		Dutch	Expansion from N.Y.	Dutch Reformed	
				English	Religious freedom	Quaker	
DELAWARE	1683	Duke of York	1638	Swedish	Economic gain	Lutheran	None
	1693	Part of Pa.		Dutch		Dutch Reformed	
	1704	Separate gov't		English		Anglican	
NORTH CAROLINA	1712	Separate gov't from S.C.	1653	English	Economic gain	Anglican	Church of England
	1729	Royal Colony					
SOUTH CAROLINA	1663	Carolina Company	1670	English	Economic gain	Anglican	Church of England (1704)
				French	Religious freedom	Huguenots	
PENNSYLVANIA	1681	William Penn	1681	English	Religious freedom	Quaker	None
				German	Fleeing Thirty Years' War	Lutheran	
				German	Religious freedom	Mennonite Brethren Amish Schwenkfelder Moravian	
GEORGIA	1732	James Oglethorpe	1733	English	Relief for those in debtors' prisons	Anglican	Church of England (1758)
	1752	Royal Colony		German	Religious freedom	Moravian	

54. Religious Utopian Communities in America

GROUP	LEADERS	LOCATION	DISTINCTIVES
ORDER OF THE SOLITARY (Ephrata Cloister)	Conrad Beissel (1690–1768) John Peter Miller (1710–1796)	Ephrata, Pa.	strict asceticism seventh-day Sabbath pacifism communalism believers' baptism
UNITED SOCIETY OF BELIEVERS IN CHRIST'S SECOND APPEARING (Shakers)	Ann Lee Stanley (1736–1784) Joseph Meacham	New Lebanon, N.Y. Union Village, Ohio 17 other communities in New England and Midwest	Mother Ann Lee's belief that she was Christ in His second coming sexual relations the root of all evil pacifism universalism communication with dead speaking in tongues group dancing (source of common name) auricular confession communalism God both male and female Millennium began in 1787
THE SOCIETY OF THE PUBLIC UNIVERSAL FRIEND	Jemima Wilkinson (1752–1819)	Lake Seneca, N.Y. Crooked Lake, N.Y.	Jemima Wilkinson's becoming the Public Universal Friend, the Publisher of Truth, after dying and having her body inhabited by the Spirit of Life Wilkinson believed to be Christ in His second coming by her followers celibacy
HARMONY SOCIETY (Rappites)	George Rapp (1757–1847)	Harmony, Pa. New Harmony, Ind. Economy, Pa.	universalism celibacy auricular confession communalism uniform dress rejection of sacraments opposition to education
COMMUNITY OF TRUE INSPIRATION (Amana Church Society)	Michael Krausert Christian Metz Barbara Heinemann	Ebenezer, N.Y. Amana, Iowa	influenced by German Pietism communalism pacifism leaders divinely inspired now a corporation
ONEIDA COMMUNITY	John Humphrey Noyes (1811–1886)	Oneida, N.Y. Wallingford, Conn.	perfectionism communal "complex marriage" procreation by communal decision on eugenic basis communalism manufacture of traps and silverware

55. The American Puritans

NAME	DATES	EDUCATION	REPRESENTATIVE WRITINGS	NOTABLE FACTS
JOHN COTTON	1584–1652	Cambridge	The Keyes of the Kingdom of Heaven The Way of the Churches of Christ in New England	Was Anglican pastor 1612–1633. Forced from England by Archbishop Laud. Served as pastor of First Congregational Church in Boston for almost 20 years. Advocated exile of Roger Williams and Anne Hutchinson.
THOMAS HOOKER	1586–1647	Cambridge		Left England because of persecution by Archbishop Laud. Spent 3 years in Holland. Accompanied Cotton to Massachusetts Bay in 1633. Moved congregation to Connecticut, founded Hartford. Helped write constitution for Connecticut colony.
RICHARD MATHER	1596–1669	Oxford	Bay Psalm Book	Was suspended from ministry by Archbishop Laud in 1633. Served as pastor at Dorchester, Mass., from 1636. Advocated Half-Way Covenant.
ROGER WILLIAMS	c.1603–c.1683	Cambridge		Was ordained in Anglican church, later moved toward Separatism. Came to New England in 1631, seeking liberty of conscience. Conflicts forced moves from Boston to Plymouth to Salem. Was expelled from Massachusetts Bay in 1635. Founded Providence, Rhode Island. Started first Baptist Church in America in 1639.

55. The American Puritans (continued)

NAME	DATES	EDUCATION	REPRESENTATIVE WRITINGS	NOTABLE FACTS
THOMAS SHEPARD	1605–1649	Cambridge	The Sincere Convert	Fled to New England in 1635 to escape Archbishop Laud. Became pastor at Cambridge, Mass. Defended American Puritans against accusations of cowardice and independency.
INCREASE MATHER	1639–1723	Harvard	A Brief History of the Wars With the Indians / An Essay for the Recording of Illustrious Providences	Was son of Richard Mather. Served as pastor in England until Restoration. Was pastor of North Church, Boston, from 1664. Advocated Half-Way Covenant. Was president of Harvard, 1684–1701.
SOLOMON STODDARD	1643–1729	Harvard	A Guide to Christ / A Treatise Concerning Conversion	Became first librarian of Harvard College. Served as pastor at Northampton, Mass., from 1670. Believed in regenerating power of Lord's Supper. Advocated Half-Way Covenant. Was grandfather of Jonathan Edwards.
COTTON MATHER	1663–1728	Harvard	Magnalia Christi Americana / Memorable Providences Relating to Witchcraft and Possessions	Was son of Increase Mather. Graduated from Harvard at age 15. Assisted father at North Church in Boston. Opposed decline of Puritan Theocracy. Advocated 1692 Salem witch trials. Was admitted to Royal Society in 1713.

56. Leaders of the First Great Awakening

NAME	DATES	COLONY	CHURCH AFFILIATION	NOTABLE FACTS
WILLIAM TENNENT	1673– 1746	Pennsylvania	Presbyterian	Was born in Ireland. Came to Philadelphia in 1717. In 1735 built "Log College" to train ministers, many of whom participated in First Great Awakening.
THEODORE J. FRELINGHUYSEN	1691– c.1748	New Jersey	Dutch Re- formed	Was born in East Friesland. Came to Raritan River area in 1720. Alienated parishioners by refusing communion to some of church's elders. Was instrumental in forming Dutch Reformed Church in America.
JONATHAN EDWARDS	1703– 1758	Massachusetts	Congregational	Was grandson of Solomon Stoddard. Knew Hebrew, Greek, and Latin when he entered Yale at age 13. Became pastor in Northampton, Mass. Served as missionary to Indians. Became president of Princeton (1758). Was possibly the greatest theologian America ever produced. Wrote *Religious Affections, The Freedom of the Will, Narrative of the Surprising Work of God.* Died of smallpox inoculation.
GILBERT TENNENT	1703– 1764	Pennsylvania New Jersey	Presbyterian	Was eldest son of William Tennent. Was trained in Log College. Worked with Frelinghuysen. Traveled with Whitefield. Preached "The Danger of an Unconverted Ministry." Helped start College of New Jersey (Princeton).
SHUBAL STEARNS	1706– 1771	Southern Colonies	Baptist	Was born in Boston. Became converted under Whitefield's preaching. In 1758 formed Baptist Association in Sandy Creek, North Carolina.

56. Leaders of the First Great Awakening (continued)

NAME	DATES	COLONY	CHURCH AFFILIATION	NOTABLE FACTS
DANIEL MARSHALL	1706– 1784	Southern Colonies	Baptist	Was born in Windsor, Connecticut. Spent 2 years as missionary to Indians. Was brother-in-law and associate of Stearns. Helped organize Georgia Baptist Association.
ELEAZER WHEELOCK	1711– 1779	Connecticut	Congregational	Graduated from Yale. Was associate of Jonathan Edwards. Was founder and first president of Dartmouth, founded to train Indians as missionaries.
HENRY MELCHIOR MUHLENBERG	1711– 1787	Pennsylvania	Lutheran	Was called Father of American Lutheranism. Was born in Hanover, Germany. Graduated from University of Göttingen. Was influenced by Pietism at Halle. Came to Pennsylvania in 1742. Formed first Lutheran Synod in America.
SAMUEL BLAIR	1712– 1751	Pennsylvania New Jersey	Presbyterian	Studied under William Tennent at Log College. Served as pastor in Pennsylvania and New Jersey. Was associate of Gilbert Tennent. Started school in Foggs Manor, Pa.
GEORGE WHITEFIELD	1714– 1770		Anglican	Was member of Holy Club at Oxford. Was early friend of Wesleys. Became most famous evangelist of his day. Made 7 trips to American colonies. Was catalyst of First Great Awakening. Knew Edwards, Frelinghuysen, Tennents.
SAMUEL DAVIES	1723– 1761	Virginia	Presbyterian	Studied under Samuel Blair. In 1747 helped form presbytery in Hanover County, Virginia. Helped found and served as president of College of New Jersey (Princeton).

57. Religious Influences Supporting the American Revolution

REASONS FOR SUPPORTING REVOLUTION	GROUPS WHO SUPPORTED REVOLUTION				
	CONGRE-GATIONALISTS	PRESBYTERIANS	ANGLICAN LAYMEN (S. Colonies)	LUTHERANS	RADICAL DISSENTERS
Covenantal view of society—a government that violates God's covenant forfeits its right to obedience	✓	✓			
Religious freedom is possible only when there is political freedom	✓	✓	✓	✓	✓
Deist emphasis on natural law and human rights			✓		
Fear of Anglican establishment, renewed persecution	✓	✓			✓
Fear of Anglican establishment, desire to see their own churches established	✓	✓		✓	
Fear of Anglican establishment, desire to minimize religious interference in political affairs			✓		
Fear of Anglican establishment, rejection of establishment as general principle					✓

58. Religious Influences Opposed to the American Revolution

REASONS FOR OPPOSING REVOLUTION	GROUPS WHO OPPOSED REVOLUTION			
	ANGLICAN CLERGY	ANGLICAN LAYMEN (NEW ENGLAND AND MIDDLE COLONIES)	RADICAL DISSENTERS	METHODISTS
Biblical requirement to submit to rulers as ordained by God	✓	✓		✓
Oath of loyalty to king sacred according to Scripture	✓			
God's favor of order of British rule over the anarchy that may replace it	✓	✓		
British rule seen as an aid to Anglican establishment	✓	✓		
Influence of John Wesley's "Calm Address to the American Colonies"				✓
Support of pacifism as a general principle			✓	

59. Leaders of the Second Great Awakening

NAME	DATES	BIRTHPLACE	CHURCH AFFILIATION	SCHOOLS FOUNDED AND/OR TAUGHT AT	NOTABLE FACTS
FRANCIS ASBURY	1745–1816	Birmingham, England	Methodist		In 1784 was appointed bishop for North America by John Wesley. Differed with Wesley over American Revolution. Pioneered circuit riding. Traveled about 300,000 miles on horseback. Methodist Church in U.S. grew by over 200,000 members under his leadership.
TIMOTHY DWIGHT	1752–1817	Northampton, Massachu-setts	Congregational	Yale College (president 1795–1817)	Was grandson of Jonathan Edwards. While at Yale started revival that soon spread to other colleges. Became poet and hymn-writer.
JAMES McGREADY	c.1758–1817	Western Pennsylvania	Presbyterian		Served as pastor in North Carolina, Kentucky. Originated camp meeting, July 1800. Helped found Cumberland Presbyterian Church.
THOMAS CAMPBELL	1763–1854	Scotland	Presbyterian		Came to America in 1807. Resigned from Presbyterian Church. Began independent ministry, which was taken over by his son; group became Disciples of Christ.
BARTON W. STONE	1772–1844	Port Tobacco, Maryland	Presbyterian		Was converted under McGready's preaching. Organized famous camp meeting in Cane Ridge, Kentucky, in 1801. Founded Christian Church, which later merged with Campbellites.
LYMAN BEECHER	1775–1863	New Haven, Connecticut	Presbyterian	Lane Theological Seminary (president 1832–1852)	Was student of Dwight at Yale. Became successful pastor and evangelist. Was noted social reformer—opposed slavery, alcoholic beverages, dueling. Helped found American Bible Society. Was father of Henry Ward Beecher and Harriet Beecher Stowe.

59. Leaders of the Second Great Awakening (continued)

NAME	DATES	BIRTHPLACE	CHURCH AFFILIATION	SCHOOLS FOUNDED AND/OR TAUGHT AT	NOTABLE FACTS
ASAHEL NETTLETON	1783–1844	North Killingworth, Connecticut	Congregational	Theological Institute of Connecticut (helped to found in 1733, lectured there occasionally)	Was called to missionary work abroad, but poor health and success in revivals at home prevented it. Began evangelistic work in rural Connecticut. Poor health forced him into semiretirement in 1820. Opposed New Haven Theology and Finney's New Measures.
BENNET TYLER	1783–1858	Connecticut	Congregational	Dartmouth College (president 1822–1828) Theological Institute of Connecticut (president 1833–1858)	Was student of Dwight at Yale. Served as pastor in Portland, Maine. Opposed innovations of New Haven Theology. Wrote biography of Nettleton.
NATHANIEL WILLIAM TAYLOR	1786–1858	New Milford, Connecticut	Congregational	Yale Divinity School (taught 1822–1858)	Was student of Dwight at Yale. Served as pastor of First Church, New Haven, Connecticut. Was major developer of New Haven Theology.
ALEXANDER CAMPBELL	1788–1866	Northern Ireland	Presbyterian	Bethany College (founder and president (1840–1866)	Was son of Thomas Campbell. Studied in Glasgow. Published periodical *Christian Baptist*. Founded Disciples of Christ. Merged with followers of Barton Stone in 1832.
CHARLES G. FINNEY	1792–1875	Warren, Connecticut	Presbyterian	Oberlin College (taught 1835–1866; president from 1851)	Was trained in law. Was converted in 1821, licensed shortly after. Originated New Measures in evangelism. Taught entire sanctification. Opposed by Beecher and Nettleton. Was an active abolitionist.

60. Major Nineteeth-Century Evangelical Social Reform Movements

REFORM MOVEMENT	KEY EVANGELICAL LEADERS	REFORM ORGANIZA- TIONS	RESULTS ACHIEVED
ABOLITION OF SLAVERY	Samuel Hopkins (1721–1803) Lyman Beecher (1775–1863) Charles G. Finney (1792–1875) John Brown (1800–1859) Theodore Weld (1803–1895) Jonathan Blanchard (1811–1892) Harriet Beecher Stowe (1811–1896)	1807—Friends of Humanity Association 1817—Colonization Society 1818—American Conventions for Promoting the Abolition of Slavery and Improving the Condition of the African Race 1833—American Anti-Slavery Society 1840—Liberty Party 1848—Free Soil Party	1861–1865—Civil War 1863—Emancipation Proclamation 1865—Thirteenth Amendment 1866—Fourteenth Amendment
PROHIBITION OF ALCOHOLIC BEVERAGES	Lyman Beecher (1775–1863) Frances Willard (1839–1898) Billy Sunday (1862–1935)	1813—Massachusetts Society for the Suppression of Intemperance 1826—American Society for the Promotion of Temperance 1836—American Temperance Union 1840—Washingtonians 1869—National Prohibition Party 1874—Women's Christian Temperance Union 1893—Anti-Saloon League	1846—Maine passed Prohibition Ordinance 1847–1855—Thirteen other states followed 1919–1932—Prohibition Amendment in force
WOMEN'S RIGHTS	Emma Willard (1787–1870) Matthew Vassar (1792–1868) Angelina Grimke (1792–1873) Mary Lyon (1797–1849)	1848—Women's Rights Convention 1869—National Woman Suffrage Association 1869—American Woman Suffrage Association 1892—Federal Woman Suffrage Association	1821—"Female Seminary" founded in Troy, New York 1836—Mt. Holyoke College founded 1861—Vassar College founded 1917—Suffrage to women granted by New York 1918—Fourteen other states followed 1920—Woman Suffrage Amendment

61. Denominational Schisms Over Slavery

DENOMINATION	YEAR OF DIVISION	NORTHERN ORGANIZATION	SOUTHERN ORGANIZATION	YEAR OF REUNION
PRESBYTERIAN	1861	Presbyterian Church in the United States of America	Presbyterian Church in the Confederate States (later Presbyterian Church in the United States)	1983
METHODIST	1844	Methodist Episcopal Church	Methodist Episcopal Church, South	1939
BAPTIST	1845	American Baptist Missionary Union (now American Baptist Convention)	Southern Baptist Convention	
EPISCOPAL	1861	Protestant Episcopal Church	Protestant Episcopal Church in the Confederate States of America	1865

62. Major Nineteenth-Century American Cults

	MORMONS	ADVENTISTS		CHRISTIAN SCIENCE	JEHOVAH'S WITNESSES
OFFICIAL NAME	Church of Jesus Christ of Latter-Day Saints	Seventh-Day Adventists		Church of Christ, Scientist	Watchtower Bible and Tract Society
FOUNDER(S)	Joseph Smith, Jr. (1805–1844)	William Miller (1782–1849) (Movement)	Former Followers of Miller (Church)	Mary Baker Glover Patterson Eddy (1821–1910)	Charles Taze Russell (1852–1916)
DATE	1830	1844	1860	1879	1884
PLACE	Harmony, Pa.	Northern N.Y.	Battle Creek, Mich.	Boston, Mass.	Pittsburgh, Pa.
OTHER MAJOR FIGURES	Brigham Young (1801–1877)	Hiram Edson Joseph Bates Ellen G. White (1827–1915)			Joseph F. Rutherford (1869–1942) Nathan H. Knorr (1905–1977)
EXTRABIBLICAL SOURCES OF AUTHORITY	*Book of Mormon* *Doctrine and Covenants* *Pearl of Great Price* Ongoing divine revelation through president of church	Writings of Ellen G. White Continuing gift of prophecy within church		*Science and Health With Key to the Scriptures*	*New World Translation of the Holy Scriptures* Writings produced by Brooklyn, N.Y., headquarters
DOCTRINE OF GOD	Polytheism—God was once man; man becomes God. God has a body.	Orthodox		Pantheism—All is God. Matter does not exist.	Monotheism—Doctrine of the Trinity is denied.
PERSON OF CHRIST	Christ is divine, but not unique.	Orthodox		Distinguish between Jesus (a man) and Christ (a divine idea) cf. Gnosticism	Arian—Christ is unique but not divine, identified with Michael the Archangel, the first created being.
WORK OF CHRIST	Death of Christ erased effect of Adam's sin, thus providing for the resurrection of all people.	Atonement is substitutionary but not finished. Investigative judgment is now determining whose sins are to be blotted out.		Christ was the great example of a scientific healing practitioner.	Ransom removes original sin from all "good and faithful" people, providing them with opportunity for everlasting life.

	MORMONS	ADVENTISTS	CHRISTIAN SCIENCE	JEHOVAH'S WITNESSES
HOLY SPIRIT	impersonal force	Orthodox	not distinguished from God	impersonal force
MAN	Man was preexistent and has innate goodness.	Orthodox (dichotomist)	Man is coeternal with God. Bodies are nonexistent. Sin is imaginary.	Sin is not pervasive, merely an imperfection.
SALVATION	Comes through faith, repentance, baptism, laying on of hands, keeping commandments.	Comes through faith, keeping Mosaic law (especially Sabbath commandment).	Comes through realizing that sin and evil do not exist.	Comes through faith plus works to gain God's approval.
CHURCH	Exclusivist—After apostle John died, church ceased to exist until 1830; only their sacraments valid.	Formerly exclusivist—Now teach that all true believers will eventually keep the Ten Commandments.	Exclusivist	Exclusivist—All others will be annihilated.
INDIVIDUAL ESCHATOLOGY	There is a second chance after death; no eternal punishment; man eventually advances to Godhood.	Soul sleep and annihilation of wicked are taught.	There is probation after death, allowing growth into truth; otherwise, annihilation.	Soul sleep and annihilation of wicked are taught.
GENERAL ESCHATOLOGY	Israel (American Indians) will be restored. Millennial reign of Christ will take place from Jerusalem and Independence, Missouri. All people will be assigned to one of three kingdoms, according to degree of spiritual advancement.	Hold premillennial, posttribulational views. Righteous will spend eternity on renewed earth.		Christ returned in 1914. Millennial kingdom was to begin after Armageddon in 1975. The 144,000 will spend eternity in heaven, all other Witnesses in earthly Paradise.
PRACTICE	Practice abstinence from liquor, tobacco, coffee, tea. Fasting, tithing, sabbath keeping are required. Marriage is for time and eternity. Encourage baptism for dead relatives.	Adhere to Old Testament dietary laws. Practice Sabbath-keeping, believers' baptism by immersion, footwashing.	Have no sacraments. Church government and teaching cannot be changed without written permission from Mrs. Eddy. All churches are linked to the Mother Church in Boston.	Teach total pacifism. Refuse to participate in government (voting, holding office, saluting flag, taking oath, etc.). No blood transfusions are permitted.

63. Late-Nineteenth- and Early-Twentieth-Century Revivalists

NAME	DATES	BIRTHPLACE	CHURCH AFFILIATION	SCHOOLS FOUNDED AND/OR TAUGHT AT	NOTABLE FACTS
DWIGHT L. MOODY	1837–1899	Northfield, Massachusetts	Independent	Northfield Seminary (school for girls; founder–1879) Mt. Hermon School (school for boys; founder–1881) Chicago Evangelization Society (now Moody Bible Institute; founder–1886)	Dropped out of school in seventh grade. Was converted at age 18. Became shoe salesman in Boston, then Chicago. Organized Sunday school in Chicago. Began preaching among soldiers during Civil War. Gained prominence with 1873–1875 crusade in the Bristish Isles. Was never ordained. Held crusades all over America until his death in 1899.
SAMUEL PORTER JONES	1847–1906	Oak Bowery, Alabama	Methodist		Never attended college. Was converted after bout with alcoholism. Supported Prohibition. Became known as the "Moody of the South."
REUBEN A. TORREY	1856–1928	Hoboken, New Jersey	Congregational	Moody Bible Institute (president 1889–1908) Bible Institute of Los Angeles (dean 1912–1924)	Graduated from Yale College and Divinity School. Worked with Moody. Made several international preaching tours.
J. WILBUR CHAPMAN	1859–1918	Richmond, Indiana	Presbyterian		Attended Oberlin College, Lake Forest University, Lane Theological Seminary. Assisted Moody in some of his crusades. Was director of Winona Lake Bible Conference.
BILLY SUNDAY	1862–1935	Ames, Iowa	Presbyterian		Was professional baseball player, 1883–1891. Was converted through Pacific Garden Mission in Chicago in 1886. Assisted J. Wilbur Chapman in some of his crusades. Began independent crusades in 1896. Had a highly sensational, dramatic preaching style. Advocated temperance. Opposed theory of evolution.

64. Key Figures in the Dissemination of Dispensationalism in America

NAME	DATES	CHURCH AFFILIATION	REPRESENTATIVE WRITINGS	SCHOOLS FOUNDED AND/OR TAUGHT AT	NOTABLE FACTS
JOHN NELSON DARBY	1800–1882	Church of Ireland Plymouth Brethren	On the Nature and Unity of the Church of Christ		Studied law. Was ordained to priesthood in 1825. Was greatest popularizer of Plymouth Brethren. Visited America seven times.
JAMES H. BROOKES	1830–1897	Presbyterian	Maranatha Israel and the Church Is the Bible Inspired?		Organized Niagara Bible Conferences. Influenced Scofield. Studied at Miami University of Ohio, Princeton Theological Seminary. Served as pastor in Dayton and St. Louis.
WILLIAM E. BLACKSTONE	1841–1935	Methodist	Jesus Is Coming		Helped start Chicago Hebrew Mission. Supported Zionism. Has forest named after him in Israel.
CYRUS INGERSON SCOFIELD	1843–1921	Congregational	Scofield Reference Bible Rightly Dividing the Word of Truth	Philadelphia School of the Bible (helped found, 1914)	Served in Confederate army. Studied law. Served in Kansas House of Representatives. Was influenced by Brookes. Served as pastor in Dallas, Tex., and Northfield, Mass. Founded Central American Mission. Spread dispensationalism through his annotated reference Bible.
ARNO C. GAEBELEIN	1861–1945	Methodist	The Annotated Bible Revelation, an Analysis and Exposition Current Events in the Light of the Bible		Was born in Germany. Founded and edited *Our Hope* magazine. Served as pastor in Baltimore, New York, Hoboken. Superintended Hope of Israel Mission.
LEWIS SPERRY CHAFER	1871–1952	Presbyterian	Systematic Theology The Kingdom in History and Prophecy Major Bible Themes	Philadelphia School of the Bible (co-founder and teacher, 1914–1923) Dallas Theological Seminary (founder and teacher, 1924–1952)	Studied music at Oberlin College. Taught at Mt. Hermon School for Boys. Served as pastor at Scofield Memorial Church in Dallas. Edited *Bibliotheca Sacra*.

65. A Comparison of Historic Covenant and Historic Dispensational Theology

ISSUE	COVENANT POSITION	DISPENSATIONAL POSITION
PATTERN OF HISTORY	Covenant of Works with Adam; Covenant of Grace with Christ on behalf of elect (some distinguish between Covenant of Redemption with Christ and Covenant of Grace with the elect).	Divided into dispensations (usually seven); e.g., Innocence (pre-Fall), Conscience (Adam), Human Government (Noah), Promise (Abraham), Law (Moses), Grace (Christ's First Coming), Kingdom (Christ's Second Coming).
VIEW OF HISTORY	Optimistic: God is extending His kingdom.	Pessimistic: the Last Days are marked by increasingly worse wickedness in the world and by apostasy in the church.
GOD'S PURPOSE IN HISTORY	There is a unified redemptive purpose.	There are two distinct purposes, one earthly (Israel), one heavenly (church).
VIEW OF THE BIBLICAL COVENANTS	They are different administrations of the Covenant of Grace.	They mark off periods of time during which God's specific demands of man differ.
RELATIONSHIP OF OLD TESTAMENT TO NEW TESTAMENT	Acceptance of Old Testament teaching required unless specifically abrogated by New Testament.	Old Testament prescriptions are not binding unless reaffirmed in New Testament.
RELATIONSHIP BETWEEN ISRAEL AND THE CHURCH	The church is spiritual Israel, in continuity with true Israel of Old Testament.	The church is the spiritual people of God, distinct from Israel, the physical people of God.
OLD TESTAMENT PROPHECY	Refers to God's people, the church.	Refers to ethnic Israel.
CHURCH AGE	God's redemptive purpose continued to unfold.	There is a parenthesis between past and future manifestations of the kingdom.
ROLE OF HOLY SPIRIT	The Holy Spirit indwells God's people throughout history.	The Holy Spirit indwells God's people only from Pentecost to the Rapture.
BAPTISM	Unified covenant generally used to support infant baptism.	Israel/church distinction often (but not always) used to support believers' baptism.
SOCIAL IMPLICATIONS	Emphasizes "cultural mandate."	The only way to save the world is to save individuals; therefore evangelism takes precedence over "social action."
ESCHATOLOGY	Usually amillennial; rarely postmillennial; occasionally premillennial.	Premillennial, usually pretribulational.
MILLENNIUM	Symbolic, often identified with present age.	Literal, earthly 1000-year reign after Second Coming.

66. Denominational Divisions Over the Modernist–Fundamentalist Controversy

DENOMINATION	YEAR OF DIVISION	SECEDING GROUP	NATURE OF SECEDING GROUP	KEY FIGURES	
				CONSERVATIVE	LIBERAL
DISCIPLES OF CHRIST	1927	North American Christian Convention of the Disciples of Christ	Conservative	Isaac Erret John W. McGarvey	James H. Garrison Herbert L. Willett
NORTHERN BAPTIST CONVENTION	1932	General Association of Regular Baptists	Conservative	John Roach Straton Jasper C. Massee Amzi C. Dixon William Bell Riley Chester Tulga Robert Ketchum	Walter Rauschenbusch Harry Emerson Fosdick
(Now American Baptist Convention)	1947	Conservative Baptist Association	Conservative		
PRESBYTERIAN CHURCH IN THE UNITED STATES OF AMERICA	1936	Orthodox Presbyterian Church	Conservative	J. Gresham Machen Paul Woolley	J. Ross Stevenson Henry Sloan Coffin
PRESBYTERIAN CHURCH IN THE UNITED STATES	1973	Presbyterian Church in America	Conservative	G. Aiken Taylor	
LUTHERAN CHURCH, MISSOURI SYNOD	1976	Association of Evangelical Lutherans	Liberal	Jacob A. O. Preus Ralph Bohlmann	John Tietjen Arlis Ehlen

67. Key Figures in the Twentieth-Century Presbyterian Schisms

NAME	DATES	SCHOOLS FOUNDED AND/OR TAUGHT AT	REPRESENTATIVE WRITINGS	NOTABLE FACTS
CHARLES A. BRIGGS	1841–1913	Union Theological Seminary (taught 1874–1913)	Hebrew and English Lexicon of the Old Testament Critical and Exegetical Commentary on the Book of Psalms	Studied at University of Virginia, Union Theological Seminary, University of Berlin. In 1893 was suspended from Presbyterian church for denying inspiration of Scripture. In 1900 was ordained in Episcopal church. Was first editor of International Critical Commentary series.
HENRY PRESERVED SMITH	1847–1927	Lane Theological Seminary (taught 1874–1894) Amherst (1898–1907) Meadville Theological School (1907–1913) Union Theological Seminary (1913–1925)	The Religion of Israel Essays in Biblical Interpretation	Studied at Amherst, Lane, Berlin. 1894 was suspended for heresy for defending Briggs.
BENJAMIN B. WARFIELD	1851–1921	Western Theological Seminary (taught 1878–1887) Princeton Theological Seminary (1887–1921)	The Plan of Salvation Counterfeit Miracles Revelation and Inspiration Perfectionism	Studied at Princeton University and Seminary. Was major opponent of Briggs and Smith. Maintained continuity of Princeton Theology from Hodges. Edited *Princeton Theological Review*.
ROBERT DICK WILSON	1856–1930	Western Theological Seminary (taught 1880–1881, 1883–1900) Princeton Theological Seminary (taught 1900–1929) Westminster Theological Seminary (cofounded and taught 1928–1930)	Hebrew Grammar for Beginners Studies in the Book of Daniel Scientific Investigation of the Old Testament	Was notable philologist and Old Testament scholar. Opposed higher criticism, defended authenticity of Old Testament documents.
HENRY SLOAN COFFIN	1877–1954	Union Theological Seminary (taught 1905–1945; president from 1926)	In a Day of Social Rebuilding The Meaning of the Cross	Wrote Auburn Affirmation. Studied at Yale, Edinburgh, Union Theological Seminary. Advocated Social Gospel. Was involved in ecumenism.

NAME	DATES	SCHOOLS FOUNDED AND/OR TAUGHT AT	REPRESENTATIVE WRITINGS	NOTABLE FACTS
HARRY EMERSON FOSDICK	1878–1969	Union Theological Seminary (taught 1909–1946)	The Modern Use of the Bible A Guide to Understanding the Bible	As liberal Baptist preacher stirred controversy in Presbyterian Church. Was pastor of Riverside Church in New York. Helped draft Auburn Affirmation.
J. GRESHAM MACHEN	1881–1937	Princeton Theological Seminary (taught 1906–1929) Westminster Theological Seminary (founded and taught 1929–1937)	Christianity and Liberalism The Virgin Birth The Origin of Paul's Religion	Studied at Johns Hopkins, Princeton University and Seminary. Founded Independent Board of Presbyterian Foreign Missions. Was defrocked for insubordination in 1935. Was leading founder of Orthodox Presbyterian Church.
J. OLIVER BUSWELL	1895–1977	Wheaton College (president 1926–1939) Faith Theological Seminary (taught 1939–1940) Shelton College (taught 1941–1955) Covenant Theological Seminary (taught 1956–1969)	A Systematic Theology of the Christian Religion	Studied at University of Minnesota, McCormick Theological Seminary, New York University. Served as army chaplain during World War I. Was involved in schisms in 1936, 1937, 1956.
CARL McINTIRE	b. 1906	Faith Theological Seminary (founded 1937) Shelton College (founded 1941)		Was involved in schisms in 1936, 1937, 1956. Founded American Council of Christian Churches to oppose National Council of Churches. Founded International Council of Christian Churches to oppose World Council of Churches. Supported Vietnam War.
ALLAN MacRAE	b. 1902	Westminster Theological Seminary (taught 1929–1937) Faith Theological Seminary (president 1937–1971) Biblical Theological Seminary (president 1971–1983)	The Gospel of Isaiah	Studied at Occidental College, Bible Institute of Los Angeles (Biola), Princeton Theological Seminary, University of Berlin. Was involved in schisms in 1936, 1937. Was editor of New Scofield Reference Bible. Served on translation team for New International Version.

68. An American Presbyterian Family Tree

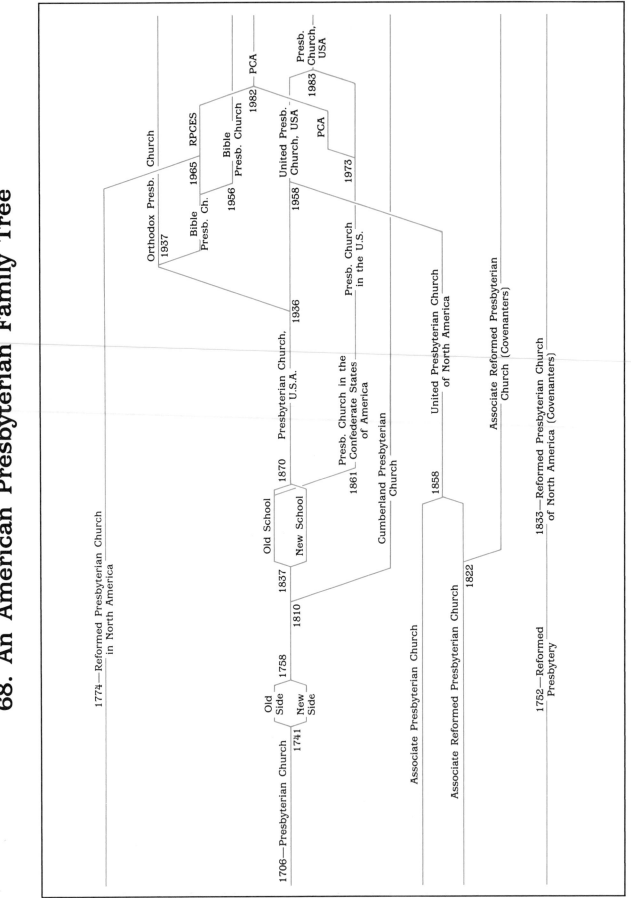

1774—Reformed Presbyterian Church in North America

Orthodox Presb. Church

1937 — Bible Presb. Ch. — 1956 — Bible Presb. Church

1965 — RPCES

1982 — PCA

1706—Presbyterian Church

Old Side 1758

1741 New Side

1810

1837 Old School

New School 1870 — Presbyterian Church, U.S.A.

1936

United Presb. Church, USA

1958

1861 — Presb. Church in the Confederate States of America — Presb. Church in the U.S.

1973 — PCA

1983 — Presb. Church, USA

Cumberland Presbyterian Church

Associate Presbyterian Church

1858 — United Presbyterian Church of North America

1822

Associate Reformed Presbyterian Church

Associate Reformed Presbyterian Church (Covenanters)

1752—Reformed Presbytery

1833—Reformed Presbyterian Church of North America (Covenanters)

69. An American Baptist Family Tree

Seventh-Day Baptists

General Association
of Separatist Baptists

Primitive Baptists

1672
1639—British
Separatists

1827

Baptist Missionary
Convention

1814

Old Lights
New Lights

1787

c. 1770

1780

1727

1845

1895

1905

National Baptist
Convention of America

National Baptist Convention of
the U.S.A., Inc.

1915

1961
Progressive
Baptist Convention

Southern Baptist
Convention

American Baptist
Association
(Landmarkers)

General Association of
Regular Baptist Churches

Conservative Baptist
Association of America

1950—American
Baptist Convention

1947

Northern Baptist
Convention

1932

1910

Free Will Baptist (North)

Free Will Baptists

North American Baptist
General Conference

Baptist General
Conference

1840

1852

European Anabaptists

70. An American Lutheran Family Tree

1820—General Synod

1867

General Council

1918

United Synod South

1863

United Lutheran Church in America

1872—American Evangelical Lutheran Church

1890—Finnish Evangelical Lutheran Church

1860—Swedish Augustana Synod

1847—Lutheran Church, Missouri Synod

1962

Lutheran Church in America

1976

Ass'n. of Evangelical Lutherans

1988
?

Various European Immigrations

1918

1917

Evangelical Lutheran Church

1896—United Evangelical Lutheran Church

1854—Iowa Synod

Buffalo Synod

Lutheran Free Church

1900—Church of the Lutheran Brethren of America

1918—Wisconsin Evangelical Lutheran Synod

1929—Apostolic Lutheran Church of America

1818—Ohio Synod

1930

1960

1963

American Lutheran Church

Evangelical Lutheran Synod

71. An American Methodist and Episcopal Family Tree

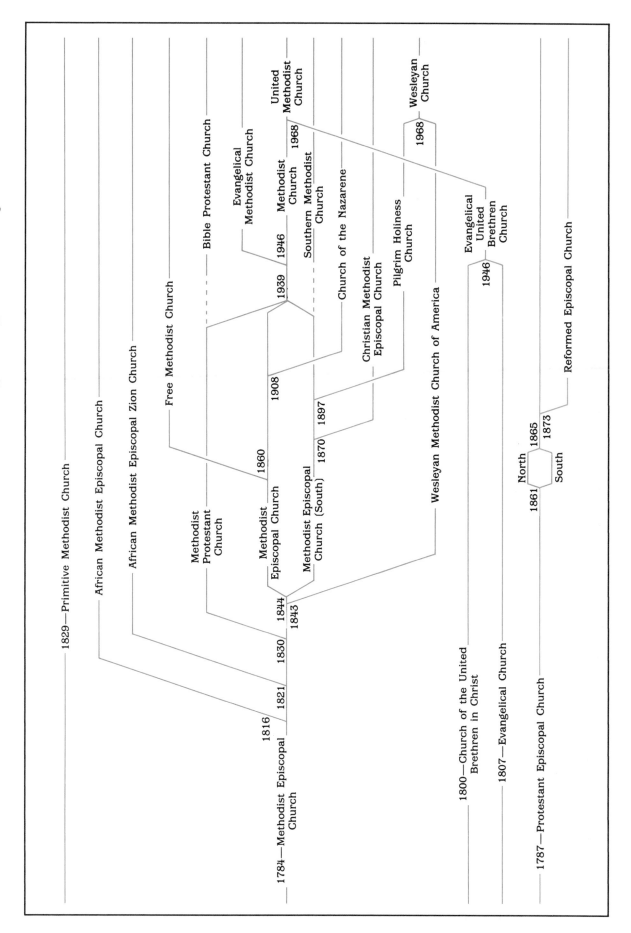

72. An American Reformed and Congregationalist Family Tree

1628—Dutch Reformed Church

1867—Reformed Church in America

1857 Christian Reformed Church

1926 Protestant Reformed Churches of America

1826—Churches of God in North America (Winebrenner)

1793 German Reformed Church

1869—Reformed Church in the U.S.

Eureka Classis

1849—Evangelical Synod of North America

1934 Evangelical and Reformed Church

1957 United Church of Christ

1801—Christians (Stone)

Churches of Christ

1807—Disciples of Christ (Campbell)

1832—Christian Church (Disciples of Christ)

Evangelical Protestant Church of North America

Congregational Christian Churches

1931

1628—Puritans

Congregationalists

1825 American Unitarian Association

1790—Universalists

Unitarian Universalist Association

1961

73. An American Pentecostal Family Tree

1886—Church of God (Cleveland, Tenn.)

1886—Church of God

1886 United Holy Church of America, Inc.

1898—Fire-baptized Holiness Church

1899—Pentecostal Holiness Church

1901—Pentecostal Union

1917—Pillar of Fire

1914—Assemblies of God, General Council

1914—Church of God by Faith, Inc.

1914—Pentecostal Assemblies of the World, Inc.

Pentecostal Assemblies of Jesus Christ, Inc.

1917—Pentecostal Church of Christ

1918—International Church of the Foursquare Gospel

1919—Pentecostal Church of God of America, Inc.

1919—International Pentecostal Assemblies

1919—Church of our Lord Jesus Christ of the Apostolic Faith, Inc.

1919—Bible Standard, Inc.

1932—Open Bible Evangelistic Association

1932—Calvary Pentecostal Church, Inc.

1947—Elim Missionary Assemblies

1923 Tomlinson Church of God

1922—Original Church of God, Inc.

1911

1918 Pentecostal Fire-baptized Holiness Church

1924 Pentecostal Church, Inc.

1945

1935 Open Bible Standard Churches, Inc.

1932

1943 — Church of God (Queens Village, N.Y.)

1957 — Church of God of All Nations

1953—Church of God of Prophecy

1953 — Emmanuel Holiness Church

United Pentecostal Church, Inc.

Bible Way Church, World-Wide

1957

HOLINESS MOVEMENT IN METHODISM

74. An American Mennonite Family Tree

1683—Mennonite Church

1872—Old Order (Wisler) Mennonite Church

1859—Church of God in Christ (Mennonite)

Old Order Amish Mennonite Church

1927

Beachy Amish Mennonite Churches

1910—Conservative Amish Mennonite Church

1954—Conservative Mennonite Conference

1812—Reformed Mennonite Church

1860—General Conference Mennonite Church

Conference of the Evangelical Mennonite Church

1865—Defenseless Mennonite Church

1876—Mennonite Brethren Church of North America

75. A Mormon Family Tree

1844 ———————Church of Jesus Christ of Latter-Day Saints (Strang)————

1860 ———Reorganized Church of Jesus Christ of Latter-Day Saints

1862 ———Church of Jesus Christ (Bickerton)

1830—Church of Jesus Christ of Latter-Day Saints

1867 ———Church of Christ (Temple Lot)————

76. An American Adventist Family Tree

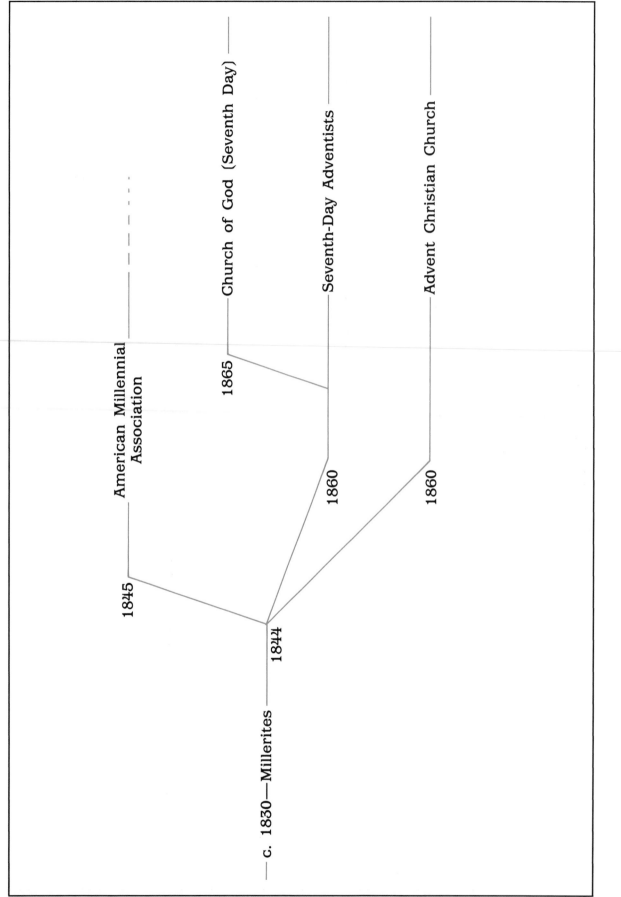

— c. 1830—Millerites

1844

1845 — American Millennial Association

1860

1865 — Church of God (Seventh Day)

1860 — Seventh-Day Adventists

1860 — Advent Christian Church

77. The Parallel Structures of Systematic Theology and Church History

OUTLINE OF SYSTEMATIC THEOLOGY	PARALLEL DEVELOPMENTS IN CHURCH HISTORY
I. Bibliology—The Doctrine of Scripture	Gnosticism and the Canon of the New Testament (2nd–4th centuries)
II. Theology Proper—The Doctrine of God III. Christology—The Doctrine of Christ IV. Pneumatology—The Doctrine of the Holy Spirit	Trinitarian Controversy (4th century) Christological Controversy (5th century)
V. Anthropology—The Doctrine of Man	Pelagian Controversy (5th–7th centuries)
VI. Soteriology—The Doctrine of Salvation	The Reformation: Protestant vs. Catholic (16th century) Reformed vs. Arminian (17th century)
VII. Ecclesiology—The Doctrine of the Church	The Reformation: Protestant vs. Catholic (16th century) Lutheran and Reformed vs. Anabaptist (16th–17th centuries)
VIII. Eschatology—The Doctrine of Last Things	Dispensationalism, Adventism, etc. (19th–20th centuries)

78. The Pendulum Effect in Church History

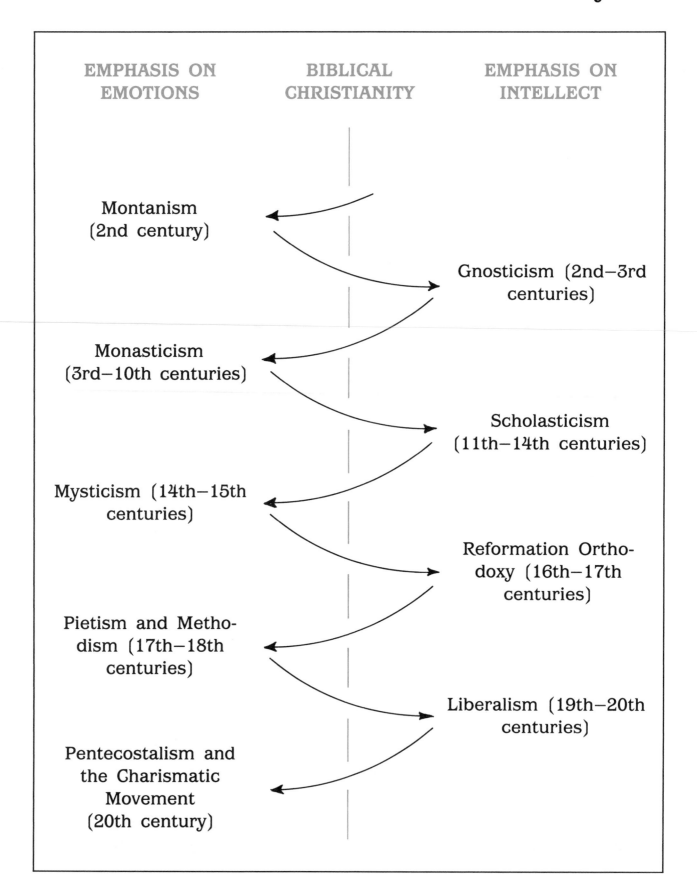

79. The Popes Recognized by the Roman Catholic Church

NAME	DATES	NAME	DATES	NAME	DATES	NAME	DATES	NAME	DATES	NAME	DATES
Peter	30–67	Simplicius	468–83	Stephen III	752–57	Gregory V	996–99	Gregory X	1272–76	Innocent IX	1591
Linus	67–76	Felix II	483–92	Paul I	757–67	Sylvester II	999–1003	Innocent V	1276	Clement VIII	1592–1605
Anacletus	76–88	Gelasius I	492–96	Stephen IV	768–72	John XVII	1003	Adrian V	1276	Leo XI	1605
Clement I	88–97	Anastasius II	496–98	Adrian I	772–95	John XVIII	1004–09	John XXI	1276–77	Paul V	1605–21
Evaristus	97–105	Symmachus	498–514	Leo III	795–816	Sergius IV	1009–12	Nicholas III	1277–80	Gregory XV	1621–23
Alexander I	105–15	Hormisdas	514–23	Stephen V	816–17	Benedict VIII	1012–24	Martin IV	1281–85	Urban VIII	1623–44
Sixtus I	115–25	John I	523–26	Paschal I	817–24	John XIX	1024–32	Honorius IV	1285–87	Innocent X	1644–55
Telesphorus	125–36	Felix III	526–30	Eugene II	824–27	Benedict IX	1032–44	Nicholas IV	1288–92	Alexander VII	1655–67
Hyginus	136–40	Boniface II	530–32	Valentine	827	Sylvester III	1045	Celestine V	1294	Clement IX	1667–69
Pius I	140–55	John II	533–35	Gregory IV	827–44	Benedict IX	1045	Boniface VIII	1294–1303	Clement X	1670–76
Anicetus	155–66	Agapitus I	535–36	Sergius II	844–47	Gregory VI	1045	Benedict XI	1303–04	Innocent XI	1676–89
Soter	166–75	Silverius	536–37	Leo IV	847–55	Clement II	1046–47	Clement V	1305–14	Alexander VIII	1689–91
Eleutherius	175–89	Vigilius	537–55	Benedict III	855–58	Benedict X	1047–48	John XXII	1316–34	Innocent XII	1691–1700
Victor I	189–99	Pelagius I	556–61	Nicholas I	858–67	Damasus II	1048	Benedict XII	1334–42	Clement XI	1700–21
Zephyrinus	199–217	John III	561–74	Adrian II	867–72	Leo IX	1049–54	Clement VI	1342–52	Innocent XIII	1721–24
Callistus I	217–22	Benedict I	575–79	John VIII	872–82	Victor II	1055–57	Innocent VI	1352–62	Benedict XIII	1724–30
Urban I	222–30	Pelagius II	579–90	Marinus I	882–84	Stephen X	1057–58	Urban V	1362–70	Clement XII	1730–40
Pontianus	230–35	Gregory I	590–604	Adrian III	884–85	Nicholas II	1059–61	Gregory XI	1370–78	Benedict XIV	1740–58
Anterus	235–36	Sabinianus	604–606	Stephen VI	885–91	Alexander II	1061–73	Urban VI	1378–89	Clement XIII	1758–69
Fabian	236–50	Boniface III	607	Formosus	891–96	Gregory VII	1073–85	Boniface IX	1389–1404	Clement XIV	1769–74
Cornelius	251–53	Boniface IV	608–15	Boniface VI	896	Victor III	1086–87	Innocent VII	1404–06	Pius VI	1775–99
Lucius I	253–54	Adeodatus I	615–18	Stephen VII	896–97	Urban II	1088–99	Gregory XII	1406–15	Pius VII	1800–23
Stephen I	254–57	Boniface V	619–25	Romanus	897	Paschal II	1099–1118	Martin V	1417–31	Leo XII	1823–29
Sixtus II	257–58	Honorius I	625–38	Theodore II	897	Gelasius II	1118–19	Eugene IV	1431–47	Pius VIII	1829–30
Dionysius	259–68	Severinus	640	John IX	898–900	Callistus II	1119–24	Nicholas V	1447–55	Gregory XVI	1831–46
Felix I	269–74	John IV	640–42	Benedict IV	900–903	Honorius II	1124–30	Callistus III	1455–58	Pius IX	1846–78
Eutychianus	275–83	Theodore I	642–49	Leo V	903	Innocent II	1130–43	Pius II	1458–64	Leo XIII	1878–1903
Caius	283–96	Martin I	649–55	Sergius III	904–11	Celestine II	1143–44	Paul II	1464–71	Pius X	1903–14
Marcellinus	296–304	Eugene I	654–57	Anastasius III	911–13	Lucius II	1144–45	Sixtus IV	1471–84	Benedict XV	1914–22
Marcellus	308–309	Vitalian	657–72	Lando	913–14	Eugene III	1145–53	Innocent VIII	1484–92	Pius XI	1922–39
Eusebius	310	Adeodatus II	672–76	John X	914–28	Anastasius IV	1153–54	Alexander VI	1492–1503	Pius XII	1939–58
Melchiades	311–14	Donus	676–78	Leo VI	928	Adrian IV	1154–59	Pius III	1503	John XXIII	1958–63
Sylvester I	314–35	Agatho	678–81	Stephen VIII	928–31	Alexander III	1159–81	Julius II	1503–13	Paul VI	1963–78
Mark	336	Leo II	682–83	John XI	931–35	Lucius III	1181–85	Leo X	1513–21	John Paul I	1978
Julius I	337–52	Benedict II	684–85	Leo VII	936–39	Urban III	1185–87	Adrian VI	1522–23	John Paul II	1978–
Liberius	352–66	John V	685–86	Stephen IX	939–42	Gregory VIII	1187	Clement VII	1523–34		
Damasus I	366–84	Cono	686–87	Marinus II	942–46	Clement III	1187–91	Paul III	1534–49		
Siricius	384–99	Sergius I	687–701	Agapitus II	946–55	Celestine III	1191–98	Julius III	1550–55		
Anastasius I	399–401	John VI	701–705	John XII	955–64	Innocent III	1198–1216	Marcellus II	1555		
Innocent I	401–17	John VII	705–707	Leo VIII	963–65	Honorius III	1216–27	Paul IV	1555–59		
Zozimus	417–18	Sisinnius	708	Benedict V	964–66	Gregory IX	1227–41	Pius IV	1559–65		
Boniface I	418–22	Constantine	708–15	John XIII	965–72	Celestine IV	1241	Pius V	1566–72		
Celestine I	422–32	Gregory II	715–31	Benedict VI	973–74	Innocent IV	1243–54	Gregory XIII	1572–85		
Sixtus III	432–40	Gregory III	731–41	Benedict VII	974–83	Alexander IV	1254–61	Sixtus V	1585–90		
Leo I	440–61	Zachary	741–52	John XIV	983–84	Urban IV	1261–64	Urban VII	1590		
Hilarus	461–68	Stephen II	752	John XV	985–96	Clement IV	1265–68	Gregory XIV	1590–91		

80. Prominent Protestant Missionaries

NAME	DATES	AREAS OF MINISTRY	HOME COUNTRY	CHURCH AFFILIATION	MISSION ORGANIZATION
JOHN ELIOT	1604–1690	North American Indians	England	Congregational	Society for the Propagation of the Gospel in New England
THOMAS BRAY	1656–1730	British North America	England	Anglican	Society for Promoting Christian Knowledge (founder) Society for the Propagation of the Gospel in Foreign Parts (founder)
BARTHOLOMAUS ZIEGENBALG	1684–1719	India	Germany	Lutheran	Danish-Halle Mission
DAVID BRAINERD	1718–1747	North American Indians	Connecticut Colony	Congregational	Scotch Society for Propagating Christian Knowledge
CHRISTIAN FRIEDRICH SCHWARTZ	1726–1798	India	Germany	Lutheran	Danish-Halle Mission
WILLIAM CAREY	1761–1834	India	England	Baptist	Baptist Missionary Society (founder)
HENRY MARTYN	1781–1812	India Persia	England	Anglican	British East India Company (chaplain)
ROBERT MORRISON	1782–1834	China	England	Anglican	London Missionary Society
ADONIRAM JUDSON	1788–1850	Burma	United States	Baptist	American Board of Commissioners for Foreign Missions (founder)
ROBERT MOFFAT	1795–1883	South Africa	Scotland	Wesleyan	London Missionary Society
ELIJAH C. BRIDGMAN	1801–1861	China	United States	Congregational	American Board of Commissioners for Foreign Missions
ALEXANDER DUFF	1806–1878	India	Scotland	Presbyterian	Church of Scotland
SAMUEL A. CROWTHER	c.1806–1891	Nigeria	Nigeria	Anglican	Church Missionary Society

80. Prominent Protestant Missionaries (continued)

NAME	DATES	AREAS OF MINISTRY	HOME COUNTRY	CHURCH AFFILIATION	MISSION ORGANIZATION
JOHANN KRAPF	1810–1881	East Africa	Germany	Lutheran	Church Missionary Society
DAVID LIVINGSTONE	1813–1873	Africa	Scotland	Independent	London Missionary Society
WILLIAM C. BURNS	1815–1868	China	Scotland	Presbyterian	English Presbyterian Church
JOHANNES REBMANN	1819–1876	East Africa	Germany	Lutheran	Church Missionary Society
JOHN G. PATON	1824–1907	New Hebrides	Scotland	Reformed Presbyterian	Reformed Presbyterian Church of Scotland
JOHN L. NEVIUS	1829–1893	China	United States	Presbyterian	Presbyterian Board of Foreign Missions
J. HUDSON TAYLOR	1832–1905	China	England	Wesleyan	China Inland Mission (founder)
H. GRATTAN GUINNESS	1835–1910	Congo	Ireland	Church of Ireland	Livingstone Inland Mission (founder) North Africa Mission (founder) Regions Beyond Missionary Union (founder)
MARY SLESSOR	1848–1915	West Africa	Scotland	Presbyterian	United Presbyterian Church of Scotland
C. T. STUDD	1862–1931	China India Congo	England	Anglican	China Inland Mission Heart of Africa Mission (founder)
ALBERT SCHWEITZER	1875–1965	French Equatorial Africa	Germany	Lutheran	Paris Society of Evangelical Missions

81. Prominent Roman Catholic Missionaries

NAME	DATES	AREAS OF MINISTRY	HOME COUNTRY	MONASTIC ORDER
BARTOLOMÉ DE LAS CASAS	1474–1566	Spanish America	Spain	Dominicans
FRANCIS XAVIER	1506–1552	India, Ceylon, East Indies, Japan	Spain	Jesuits
FRANCIS SOLANUS	1549–1610	Spanish America	Spain	Franciscans
MATTEO RICCI	1552–1610	China	Italy	Jesuits
ROBERT DE NOBILI	1577–1656	India	Italy	Jesuits
ALEXANDER DE RHODES	b.1591	Vietnam	France	Jesuits
JOHANN ADAM SCHALL VON BELL	1591–1666	China	Germany	Jesuits
GUGLIELMO MASSAJA	1809–1889	Ethiopia	Italy	Capuchins
THEOPHILE VERBIST	1823–1868	Mongolia	Belgium	Scheutveld Fathers (founder)
CHARLES M. A. LAVIGERIE	1825–1892	North Africa	France	White Fathers (founder)
JOSEPH DAMIEN DE VEUSTER	1840–1889	Hawaii	Belgium	Picpus Fathers
CHARLES EUGENE DE FOUCAULD	1858–1916	North Africa	France	Trappists

82. Major Indigenous Christian Religious Movements in Africa

NAME OF MOVEMENT	NAME OF LEADER	CHURCH AFFILIATION	DATE OF ORIGIN	GEOGRAPHICAL AREA	DISTINCTIVES
ETHIOPIAN CHURCH	Mangena M. Mokone	Wesleyan	1892	South Africa	Opposition to European control in African church
AMA-SIRAYELI (Israelites)	Enoch Mgijima	Anglican	1910	South Africa	Halley's Comet a sign to the church Rejection of New Testament, return to Old Testament roots Faith healing
HARRIS CHRISTIANS	William Wadé Harris	Methodist	1913	Ivory Coast Liberia Gold Coast	Faith healing Destruction of fetishes
MALAKITES	Malaki Musaja-kawa	Anglican	1913	Uganda	Rejection of doctors and medicine Encouragement of polygamy
	Garrick Sokari Braid	Anglican	c.1916	Nigeria	Self-designation: Second Elijah Supernatural visions Faith healing Rejection of doctors and medicine Prohibition of alcoholic beverages
KIMBANGUIST CHURCH	Simon Kimbangu	Baptist	1921	Congo	Faith healing Destruction of fetishes Rejection of polygamy

83. Translations of the Bible Into English

TRANSLATION	DATE	TRANSLATORS	COMMENTS
WYCLIFFE BIBLE	1380–1384	John Wycliffe and associates	Based on Latin Vulgate
TYNDALE BIBLE	1525–1530	William Tyndale	N.T. and Pentateuch; based on original-language MSS
COVERDALE BIBLE	1535	Miles Coverdale	Completion of Tyndale's work
MATTHEW'S BIBLE	1537	John Rogers	Used work of Tyndale and Coverdale
GREAT BIBLE	1539	Miles Coverdale	Revision of Matthew's Bible commissioned by Henry VIII
GENEVA BIBLE	1560	English Puritans in Geneva	Revision of Great Bible with Calvinistic notes
BISHOPS' BIBLE	1568	Matthew Parker and others	Revision of Great Bible; reaction against Puritanism of Geneva Bible
RHEIMS–DOUAI VERSION	1582–NT 1610–OT	Gregory Martin and other English Catholic scholars	Roman Catholic, based on Latin Vulgate, produced by English College in Rheims and later Douai
AUTHORIZED VERSION (King James Version)	1604–1611	54 English scholars of varying theological convictions	Commissioned by James I after Hampton Court Conference of 1604; elevated prose designed for oral reading; based on Textus Receptus
CHALLONER REVISION	1749–1750	Richard Challoner	Roman Catholic revision of Rheims–Douai Version; language similar to that of KJV
ALFORD TRANSLATION	1861–NT 1869–OT	Henry Alford	Produced by Dean of Canterbury Cathedral
DARBY TRANSLATION	1871	John Nelson Darby	Translation by early Plymouth Brethren leader and originator of dispensationalism
ENGLISH REVISED VERSION	1881–1885	65 English scholars of varying theological convictions	Used textual principles of Westcott and Hort; very literal.
AMERICAN STANDARD VERSION	1901	American scholars working concurrently with English translators of Revised Version	Slight modification of English Revised Version, reflecting preferences of American scholars
THE NEW TESTAMENT IN MODERN SPEECH	1903	Richard F. Weymouth	Translation by a scholar of classical Greek
A NEW TRANSLATION OF THE BIBLE	1913–NT 1924–OT	James Moffatt	Free translation, not always faithful to text, very popular in Britain
THE COMPLETE BIBLE: An American Translation	1923–NT 1927–OT	J. M. P. Smith E. J. Goodspeed	Highly readable translation by two American scholars
KNOX VERSION	1944–NT 1949–OT	Ronald Knox	Roman Catholic, based on Vulgate

83. Translations of the Bible Into English (continued)

TRANSLATION	DATE	TRANSLATORS	COMMENTS
REVISED STANDARD VERSION	1946—NT 1952—OT	32 American scholars, largely ecumenical in outlook	Sponsored by National Council of Churches; revision of the American Standard Version
THE NEW TESTAMENT: A New Translation in Plain English	1952	C. K. Williams	Emphasized simplicity of vocabulary
NEW WORLD TRANSLATION OF THE HOLY SCRIPTURES	1955 (revised 1961)	Nathan H. Knorr Frederick W. Franz and others	Jehovah's Witnesses translation, emphasizing their theological distinctives
THE NEW TESTAMENT IN MODERN ENGLISH	1958 (revised 1972)	J. B. Phillips	Free translation, lively language
BERKELEY VERSION	1945—NT 1959—OT	Gerrit Verkuyl (NT) 20 conservative scholars (OT)	Compiled in Berkeley, Calif.; also known as Modern Language Bible
AMPLIFIED BIBLE	1958—NT 1965—OT	12 editors	Produced in California; a smorgasbord of variant wordings
JERUSALEM BIBLE	1966	Roman Catholic School of Biblical Studies in Jerusalem	First Catholic Bible in English to rely extensively on original-language MSS
BARCLAY NEW TESTAMENT	1969	William Barclay	Translation by popular British preacher and writer
NEW ENGLISH BIBLE	1961—NT 1970—OT	C. H. Dodd and other British scholars of varying theological convictions	Sponsored by churches and Bible societies in Great Britain; makes extensive use of textual emendations
NEW AMERICAN BIBLE	1970	Catholic scholars of the Episcopal Confraternity of Christian Doctrine	Revision of Confraternity Version, more formal than Jerusalem Bible
NEW AMERICAN STANDARD BIBLE	1963—NT 1971—OT	Evangelical scholars	Revision of American Standard Version; sponsored by Lockman Foundation; most literal of mid-twentieth-century translations
LIVING BIBLE	1971	Kenneth Taylor	Loose but highly readable paraphrase
GOOD NEWS BIBLE (Today's English Version)	1966—NT 1976—OT	Robert Bratcher	Sponsored by American Bible Society; uses principle of "dynamic equivalence"; simplified vocabulary
NEW INTERNATIONAL VERSION	1973—NT 1978—OT	Edwin Palmer and 115 other evangelical scholars	Sponsored by the New York Bible Society (now the International Bible Society); translators from many English-speaking countries; combines accuracy and readability
NEW KING JAMES VERSION	1982	Arthur L. Farstad and 130 other evangelical scholars	Sponsored by Thomas Nelson Publishers; update of KJV, using Textus Receptus
READER'S DIGEST BIBLE	1982	Bruce Metzger and others	Condensed to about 60% of original length; reflects critical scholarship in introductions

84. Notable Protestant Historians of the Church

NAME	DATES	BIRTHPLACE	CHURCH AFFILIATION	PERIOD CHRONICLED	REPRESENTATIVE HISTORICAL WORKS
JOHN FOXE	1516–1587	Lincolnshire, England	Anglican	Early church to 1556, concentrating on Marian persecution in England	The Acts and Monuments of the Church (Foxe's Book of Martyrs)
MATTHIAS FLACIUS ILLYRICUS	1520–1575	Illyria	Lutheran	Complete to Reformation	The Magdeburg Centuries (editor)—13 vols.
COTTON MATHER	1663–1728	Boston, Massachusetts	Congregational	17th-century Puritan New England	Magnalia Christi Americana
J. A. W. NEANDER	1789–1850	Göttingen, Germany	Lutheran	Complete	General History of the Christian Religion and Church—6 vols.
J. H. MERLE D'AUBIGNE	1794–1872	Geneva, Switzerland	Evangelical Church of Switzerland	Reformation	History of the Reformation of the Sixteenth Century—5 vols. History of the Reformation in Europe at the Time of Calvin—8 vols. History of the Reformation in England—2 vols.
WILLIAM CUNNINGHAM	1805–1861	Hamilton, Scotland	Free Church of Scotland	History of Theology	Historical Theology The Reformers and the Theology of the Reformation
PHILIP SCHAFF	1819–1893	Chur, Switzerland	German Reformed	Apostolic Age Through Reformation	History of the Christian Church—8 vols. The Creeds of Christendom—3 vols.
ADOLF VON HARNACK	1851–1930	Dorpat, Estonia	Lutheran	Ante-Nicene Period	History of Dogma The Mission and Expansion of Christianity in the First Three Centuries
WILLISTON WALKER	1860–1922	Portland, Maine	Congregational	Complete	History of the Christian Church A History of the Congregational Churches in the United States The Reformation
WILLIAM W. SWEET	1881–1959	Baldwin, Kansas	Methodist	American Church History	The Story of Religion in America Religion on the American Frontier Methodism in American History
KENNETH SCOTT LATOURETTE	1884–1968	Oregon	Baptist	Complete	A History of Christianity History of the Expansion of Christianity—7 vols. Christianity in a Revolutionary Age—5 vols.

Bibliography

Abbott, Walter M., ed. *The Documents of Vatican II.* New York: Guild, 1966.

Ahlstrom, Sydney E. *A Religious History of the American People.* Garden City, N.Y.: Doubleday, Image, 1975.

Alexander, Archibald. *The Log College.* London: Banner of Truth, 1968.

Alexander, David, and Patricia Alexander, eds. *Eerdmans' Handbook to the Bible.* Grand Rapids: Eerdmans, 1973.

Aquinas, Thomas. *Summa Theologica.* New York: Benziger Brothers, 1947.

Arnold, Eberhard. *The Early Christians After the Death of the Apostles.* Rifton, N.Y.: Plough, 1970.

Ayer, Joseph Cullen. *A Source Book for Ancient Church History.* New York: Scribner, 1913.

Bainton, Roland H. *Here I Stand.* New York: New American Library, 1950.

_____. *The Reformation of the Sixteenth Century.* Boston: Beacon, 1952.

Berkhof, Louis. *The History of Christian Doctrines.* Grand Rapids: Baker, 1976.

Berry, W. Grinton, ed. *Foxe's Book of Martyrs.* Grand Rapids: Baker, 1978.

Boer, Harry R. *A Short History of the Early Church.* Grand Rapids: Eerdmans, 1976.

Brauer, Jerald C. *Protestantism in America.* Philadelphia: Westminster, 1953.

Brauer, Jerald C., ed. *The Westminster Dictionary of Church History.* Philadelphia: Westminster, 1971.

Bromiley, Geoffrey W. *Historical Theology—An Introduction.* Grand Rapids: Eerdmans, 1978.

Bruce, F. F. *The Spreading Flame.* Grand Rapids: Eerdmans, 1979.

Cairns, Earle E. *Christianity Through the Centuries.* Grand Rapids: Zondervan, 1981.

Cantor, Norman F., ed. *The Medieval World: 300–1300.* New York: Macmillan, 1963.

Chadwick, Henry. *The Early Church.* Harmondsworth, Middlesex, England: Penguin, 1967.

Chadwick, Owen. *The Reformation.* Harmondsworth, Middlesex, England: Penguin, 1964.

Corbett, James A. *The Papacy—A Brief History.* Princeton: Van Nostrand, 1956.

Coulson, John, ed. *The Saints.* New York: Guild, 1958.

Cragg, Gerald R. *The Church and the Age of Reason 1648–1789.* Harmondsworth, Middlesex, England: Penguin, 1970.

Dallimore, Arnold A. *George Whitefield.* Westchester, Ill.: Simon & Schuster, Cornerstone, 1979.

D'Aubigne, J. H. Merle. *The Life and Times of Martin Luther.* Chicago: Moody, 1978.

Dickens, A. G. *The Counter Reformation.* New York: Harcourt, Brace, and World, 1969.

_____. *Reformation and Society in Sixteenth-Century Europe.* New York: Harcourt, Brace, and World, 1966.

Dolan, John P. *History of the Reformation.* New York: New American Library, 1965.

Douglas, J. D., ed. *The New International Dictionary of the Christian Church.* Grand Rapids: Zondervan, 1974.

Dowley, Tim, ed. *Eerdmans' Handbook to the History of Christianity.* Grand Rapids: Eerdmans, 1977.

Durant, Will. *The Age of Faith.* New York: Simon and Schuster, 1950.

_____. *Caesar and Christ.* New York: Simon and Schuster, 1944.

_____. *The Reformation.* New York: Simon and Schuster, 1957.

_____. *The Renaissance.* New York: Simon and Schuster, 1953.

Elton, G. R., ed. *Renaissance and Reformation: 1300–1648.* New York: Macmillan, 1963.

Estep, William R. *The Anabaptist Story.* Grand Rapids: Eerdmans, 1975.

The Family Tree—A Chart of Protestant Denominations in the United States. Philadelphia: Eternity Magazine, 1983.

Farrar, Frederic W. *Lives of the Fathers.* New York: Macmillan, 1889.

Fremantle, Anne, ed. *A Treasury of Early Christianity.* New York: New American Library, 1953.

Gaines, David P. *The World Council of Churches.* Peterborough, N.H.: Richard R. Smith, 1966.

Gaustad, Edwin Scott. *A Religious History of America.* New York: Harper & Row, 1974.

Glover, Robert H. *The Progress of World-Wide Missions.* New York: Harper & Row, 1960.

Groves, C. P. *The Planting of Christianity in Africa.* London: Lutterworth, 1955.

Hawes, Stephen. *Synchronology of the Principal Events in Sacred and Profane History From the Creation of Man to the Present Time.* Boston: Hawes. 1870.

Hay, Denys. *The Medieval Centuries.* New York: Harper & Row, 1964.

Hildebrand, Hans J., ed. *The Reformation.* Grand Rapids: Baker, 1978.

Houghton, S. M., ed. *Five Pioneer Missionaries.* London: Banner of Truth, 1965.

_____. *Sketches From Church History.* Edinburgh: Banner of Truth, 1980.

Hughes, Philip. *A Popular History of the Reformation.* Garden City, N.Y.: Doubleday, 1957.

Kelly, J. N. D. *Early Christian Doctrines.* San Francisco: Harper & Row, 1978.

Latourette, Kenneth Scott. *A History of Christianity.* New York: Harper & Row, 1953.

_____. *A History of the Expansion of Christianity.* Grand Rapids: Zondervan, 1970.

Lebreton, Jules, and Jacques Zeiller. *The Triumph of Christianity.* New York: Collier, 1946.

McBirnie, William Steuart. *The Search for the Twelve Apostles.* Wheaton: Tyndale, 1973.

McConnell, S. D. *History of the American Episcopal Church.* New York: Thomas Whittaker, 1890.

Mead, Frank S. *Handbook of Denominations in the United States.* Nashville: Abingdon, 1975.

Miller, Perry, ed. *The American Puritans*. Garden City, N.Y.: Doubleday, 1956.

Moyer, Elgin S. *The Wycliffe Biographical Dictionary of the Church*. Chicago: Moody, 1982.

Neill, Stephen. *A History of Christian Missions*. Harmondsworth, Middlesex, England: Penguin, 1964.

Neve, J. L. *Churches and Sects of Christendom*. Burlington, Iowa: Lutheran Literary Board, 1940.

Newman, A. *A Manual of Church History*. Philadelphia: The American Baptist Publication Society, 1931.

Newton, Eric, and William Neil. *2000 Years of Christian Art*. New York: Harper & Row, 1966.

Nichols, James Hastings. *History of Christianity 1650–1950*. New York: Ronald, 1956.

Noll, Mark A. *Christians in the American Revolution*. Washington, D.C.: Christian University Press, 1977.

Noll, Mark A., et al., eds. *Eerdmans' Handbook to Christianity in America*. Grand Rapids: Eerdmans, 1983.

Parker, Percy Livingstone, ed. *The Journal of John Wesley*. Chicago: Moody, n.d.

Renwick, A. M. *The Story of the Church*. Leicester, England: InterVarsity, 1958.

Ryle, J. C. *Christian Leaders of the 18th Century*. Edinburgh: Banner of Truth, 1978.

Schaff, Philip. *History of the Christian Church*. Grand Rapids: Eerdmans, 1910.

Smith, M. A. *From Christ to Constantine*. Downers Grove, Ill.: InterVarsity, 1971.

———. *The Church Under Siege*. Downers Grove, Ill.: InterVarsity, 1976.

Southern, R. W. *Western Society and the Church in the Middle Ages*. Harmondsworth, Middlesex, England: Penguin, 1970.

Sparks, Jack, ed. *The Apostolic Fathers*. Nashville, Tenn.: Thomas Nelson, 1978.

Spitz, Lewis W., ed. *The Protestant Reformation*. Englewood Cliffs, N.J.: Prentice-Hall, 1966,

Steinberg, S. H. *Historical Tables*. London: Macmillan, 1939.

Sweet, William W. *The Story of Religion in America*. Grand Rapids: Baker, 1973.

Van Baalen, Jan Karel. *The Chaos of Cults*. Grand Rapids: Eerdmans, 1962.

Vidler, Alec R. *The Church in an Age of Revolution*. Harmondsworth, Middlesex, England: Penguin, 1961.

Westcott, B. F. *A General Survey of the History of the Canon of the New Testament*. Grand Rapids: Baker, 1980.

Workman, Herbert B. *Persecution in the Early Church*. London: Charles H. Kelly, 1906.

Index